Brad Steiger Predicts the Future

Other Brad Steiger books published by Para Research

True Ghost Stories
Astral Projection
Kahuna Magic
Monsters Among Us

Brad Steiger
Predicts the Future

1469 Morstein Road
West Chester, Pennsylvania 19380 USA

Brad Steiger Predicts the Future
by Brad Steiger

Library of Congress Catalog Card Number: 83-63065
International Standard Book Number: 0-914918-37-0

Typeset in 10 pt. Garth Graphic on Compugraphic 8400
Printed by W.P. on 55-pound Natural shade offset paper.
Edited by Shaun Levesque and Marah Ren
Cover design by Ralph Poness
Cover illustration by Todd Sweet
Graphics by Robert Killam
Typeset by Patrice LeBlanc

Published by Whitford Press
Distributed by Schiffer Publishing, Ltd.

This book may be purchased from the publisher.
Please include $2.00 postage.
Try your bookstore first.
Please send for free catalog to:
Whitford Press
c/o Schiffer Publishing, Ltd.
1469 Morstein Road
West Chester, Pennsylvania 19380

Manufactured in the United States of America

Second Printing, July 1987, 2,000 copies.
Total copies in print, 6,000

Contents

Introduction

Yₒu really can create your own tomorrow.

Hundreds of men and women have done so and discovered the wealth, good health, and happy, peaceful life that is available to all of us. Some want to know when to buy and sell on the stock market. Others wish to learn where and when droughts and famines will occur. Still others are concerned about where the "safe" places will be if societal or geological upheavals occur and shatter the world as we now perceive it.

You have your own reasons for reading this book. Whatever those reasons are, I assure you that there is a new Golden Age awaiting humankind if only men and women will seek to attain it. The current economic woes, the civil strife, the wars and rumors of wars will be replaced by an unrivaled renaissance for a global humanity, if enough of us want to make it happen.

When I say that it is possible to create your own tomorrow, I mean that literally, not mystically; and I am not speaking about the necessity of your being transformed into a Nostradamus or a berobed prophet.

There are two primary ways to make accurate predictions of the future: (1) By having a knowledge of the cycles of history and of weather; (2) By developing the ability to practice creative visualization.

Regarding the first method, history really does repeat itself. Oh, I don't mean the complete program and players. I don't mean Rome will return and the Caesars will reign on the Potomac. But I do most certainly mean that the cycles of time repeat themselves with astonishing accuracy – right down to the length of hemlines, the styling of hair and the curse of famine.

In the early 1970s, I was given access to an enormous amount of scientific research on the historical cycles of weather and energy that had been compiled by an astronomer, Selby Maxwell, and the cultural research of psychologist Raymond Wheeler. These men, who died many years ago, had actually become cartographers of Time and had fashioned a map of the future. The events of the 1980s – economic chaos, civil strife, deterioration of the existing order – have held no surprises for me. I saw them all as they were detailed on Maxwell and Wheeler's "Roadmap of Time."

John Cejka, the president of Cyclomatic Engineering of Glenview, Illinois, helped me to make sense of the thousands of documents that had been bequeathed to an unappreciative, and largely unknowing, public by these two dedicated scientists, and an extensive presentation of the Maxwell-Wheeler research material was published by me at that time. *A Roadmap of Time* (Prentice-Hall, 1975) has long been out of print; but the distillation of this and other material is what will allow you to understand how to create your own tomorrow.

In addition to this important data on how to interpret correctly the cycles of Time, I am supplying you with numerous exercises in creative visualization, which will enable you to envision scenes from your own future.

How can meditation and creative visualization permit one to create his or her own tomorrow?

It might be said that meditative practices allow us to create a positive attitude toward tomorrow and enable us to deal with our challenges as victors rather than as helpless victims of circumstances beyond our control. If that alone were true, I am certain that you would agree that would be reason enough to begin meditating and to undertake creative visualization practice; however, I am again being quite literal in asserting that creative visualization can actually grant you complete access to the doors of the future.

Some parapsychologists have stated that for one level of our consciousness, Time exists as an Eternal Now. When one learns how to shut out the external distractions of the material world, he or she can rise to an "in-between" level of awareness where the person may view the future as easily as the past. In that way, a person can acquire a "memory" of tomorrow.

This book is arranged in two sections, one for each of the methods you can use to create a happy, healthful, and prosperous future. I strenuously urge you to understand thoroughly the first section before you begin your personal experiments with the second.

I have always been a passionate student of history. I have sought since childhood to accumulate as much knowledge of this material plane as possible. My tastes have always been eclectic and universal. I have never limited my interests to one or two areas of human endeavor.

The intellect is one of our most accessible guides through the physical world in which our Souls have placed us. I have striven always to achieve a balance between the brain and the mind-soul. And I believe that if you sincerely seek to balance a thorough knowledge of the cycles of Time with an ability to practice creative visualization, you will be able to create your own tomorrow.

Part One

*Understanding the Cycles
of Time: Key to Survival*

1

The Weather-Energy Cycles

Such things as war, depressions, civil riots and stock-market crashes are considered blights that occur without structure or demonstrable pattern. But science is founded on the repeatability of experiments; religion is built on the promise of plan and order. Something within us seems to drive us to find patterns in our world, in our universe.

In the 1980s we have permitted ourselves the luxury of believing that we have largely emancipated ourselves from the forces of environment. We live in temperature-controlled homes, in which climate has been stabilized. Gravity bothers us very little, for our modern inventions permit us to circumvent its effects with ease. Although once in a great while someone may be struck by lightning, consider the many ways in which we have succeeded in harnessing the force of electricity.

But an increasing amount of evidence has been steadily accumulating that we are not as emancipated from our environment as we have thought.

From many recognized studies, we can gather the following information:

When temperatures are excessively high and the barometer is going down, people become depressed, dull, tired and absent-minded. More articles are left in stores or on trains and buses in hot, humid weather. People are more forgetful, more irritable, less tolerant of one another. Their nerves are on edge. People are more pessimistic; they have less self-confidence and "drive." They are more impulsive and subject to compulsive behavior.

At such times more accidents occur on the street, in cars, in homes, in shops and in factories. When it is hot and humid, you are more likely to cut your thumb or break a dish. A factory worker is more likely to get caught in machinery. Coordination is poorer. Typists will hit more wrong keys and make more mistakes in their spelling.

During hot and humid weather there are more violent episodes among the patients in mental hospitals. Patients in general hospitals do not feel as well. More people become sick, more sick people die.

Children are restless in school; they cannot concentrate; their minds wander; they are more irritable, less obedient and less cooperative. Teachers are lethargic, less patient and less understanding.

More people faint in hot, muggy weather. People cannot hold their liquor as well.

If you can help it, do not go to the dentist on a hot, muggy afternoon. The drill will hurt more. Don't make an important sales call; you will meet with greater resistance. People are less suggestible, more prone to find fault, and more likely to be suspicious.

Decisions made by executives are not likely to be as good because people are more erratic and less careful in their thinking in hot weather. They are more emotional and less rational. When civil service tests are taken in August, only 58 percent pass. Seventy-five percent of the applicants are successful when they take their test in April or November.

Sixty-nine percent more New Yorkers are arrested for assault and battery when the temperature is between 80° and 85° than on cool days. Crimes against persons are of greater frequency and violence during warm weather, warm seasons, years or decades. There is more crime against property during cool times.

But how far can these observations take us?

Astronomer Selby Maxwell, former science editor of the Chicago *Tribune,* discovered a weather-energy cycle that has proved to be the basic cycle which governs all weather—past, present and future. Maxwell determined the correct time lags that cause the turbulent upper air masses to act in a predetermined manner.

Crucial to Maxwell's method for predicting the weather was his revelation that all cycles of the same length turn at the same time, and that all cycles are related in one way or another to this basic energy cycle.

Professor Raymond Wheeler, who was head of the psychology department at the University of Kansas, invested over twenty years' time and the efforts of a staff of over two hundred to compile detailed records of three thousand years of weather and the apparent cycles that run through them. Nearly two million separate pieces of information about weather in history were entered on cards and supplemented with maps and charts.

Wheeler was able to chart types of governments, human achievements, wars and shifts in cultural styles from one extreme to another and back again. He was able to isolate definite patterns of human behavior, as men and women reacted to climate changes.

Wheeler discovered a one-hundred-year cycle, divided into four almost equal parts, which demonstrates that people behave differently – but predictably – during periods of warm-wet, warm-dry, cold-wet, and cold-dry weather. Wars, depressions, revolutions, cataclysmic events – together with tastes in architecture, musical expression, poetic meter and the length of hemlines – have occurred at evenly spaced intervals. Wheeler's monumental research provides demonstrable bases for predicting what will happen in years ahead.

If you were to place the Wheeler curve over the Maxwell weather-energy cycle, you would see that they match. If you then placed the weather curve established by Dr. A. E. Douglass, who studied one million rings from fifteen-hundred-year-old Arizona yellow pines in order to derive a weather "diary" from the natural records of plant growth, you would find that this pattern matches the other two.

Together, the Maxwell-Wheeler discoveries of weather-energy cycles and human ecology quite literally present us with a roadmap of time.

By *combining* the Wheeler-Maxwell curves we can foretell the most desirable date to plan a picnic, plant potatoes, buy or sell stocks, the most desirable date for practically anything.

We are not simply talking about when it will rain or snow – although in a time of impending famine, that in itself is vital information. Rather, the weather, the migratory patterns of birds, the breeding habits of mollusks, the waging of war, the price of commodities, the length of hair over the ears, virtually every single enterprise and endeavor has its own cycle. Each of these cycles, in turn, is interrelated and affected by the basic energy cycle.

Futurist, economist, advisor to the Congressional Office of Technological Assessment, and author of *Creating Alternative Futures: The End of Economics,* Hazel Henderson has expressed her opinion that the notion of linear progress is really quite new. The linear concept of time is only about three hundred years old and probably developed with the Enlightenment and the scientific revolution, which began with Descartes.

Ms. Henderson has said that "What we are seeing now is all a part of a yearning to go back to a more cyclic understanding of time. I suspect that this is one of the reasons why so many people are aware now of how much we can draw on oriental traditions, and how eastern concepts of time and space can be very helpful to us."

By recognizing that patterns of time do recur at rhythmic intervals, we can chart danger periods for our government. We can organize business, labor and governmental agencies to produce and to distribute goods according to the best periods for growth.

We can plan ahead for droughts and famines and store foodstuffs for the lean years. We can attempt to stockpile goods for periods of depression and inflation.

And for the materialistically minded, the Maxwell-Wheeler curves also parallel – and therefore can be used to predict – stock-market fluctuations. Business cycles are integrated with the entire cultural pattern and cannot fully be explained without reference to that pattern. Whatever factors set in motion the fluctuations of the culture pattern are also the factors that trigger the general prosperity-depression pattern. Business cycles have been integrated with weather trends throughout history; they still are. The Maxwell weather-energy cycle and the Wheeler culture curve combine to provide a remarkable predictor of the business cycles of all nations.

2

An Accurate Science of Forecasting

According to the theories of Selby Maxwell, long-range weather forecasting is an exact science. Systems of weather prediction utilized by the Weather Bureau are based on observation, on information from reporting stations and on the sciences of meteorology and astronomy. But Maxwell discovered what he believed to be the primary weather-energy cycle that governs all weather – past, present and future. All cycles of the same length turn at the same time, and all cycles are related in some way to the Maxwell cycle.

The Maxwell cycle is based on the movements of the Earth, Moon and Sun – but chiefly on the interaction of the Moon and the Earth. Maxwell stressed that as the Moon and Earth revolve, there is a differential in the pull of gravity. Since the Moon orbits the Earth in an ellipse, there must be a period when the Earth travels at a faster speed, and another time when it slows down. Everything on Earth is constantly subjected to two forces – the gravitational forces and the centrifugal forces from the spin of the Earth on its axis.

Ever since our early school days we have been told about tides and the Moon. The key to an understanding of the tides lies in the laws of gravitation.

The gravitational pull of the Sun, most massive of all bodies in our solar system, holds Earth in its orbit. The Moon is about 1/80th the size of the Earth, but because it is so much closer to Earth than is the Sun (250,000 miles, opposed to 92 million miles), it is held in tight gravitational bondage to Earth, a much smaller body than the Sun. But both the Sun and Moon have their own effect on the Earth; they control the Earth's tides, which wreak subtle devastation on the Earth's land mass.

When the Moon is aligned with Sun and Earth at New Moon or Full Moon, the tides are greater, because the Sun and the Moon cooperate in raising them (spring or flood tides). If, however, the Moon and the Sun are at right angles to Earth, as happens during the first or third quarters, then the two are opposed, thus raising smaller tides (neap tides).

The Moon rotates around the Earth approximately every twenty-nine and one-half days. Since Earth is also rotating, one might suppose that each location on the planet should have two high tides and two low tides each day. This is not so for several reasons.

The Moon moves in a plane more in line with the Earth's orbital plane than with the equator. In effect, Earth's axis is tilted toward the Moon. Thus at times the peak of the tidal bulge is almost 29° north of the equator, or nearly a third of the way toward the pole. Farther north than this, only one large and one small tide are observed each day.

Earth is not a smooth ball. It is rough and flecked with great ocean depths and continents. The coastlines are irregular and cannot be easily defined. The waters possess natural wave motions that tend to interfere with the tidal movements. The bottom of the ocean has a frictional drag on the water. The result of these factors, Selby Maxwell found, is that theoretical calculations must be modified by intense observation of past tidal events.

The Moon comes closer to Earth (perigee), goes farther away to its furthermost position (apogee), then comes nearer again – an irregular orbit producing a 20 percent change in tidal events.

Scientists learned long ago how to calibrate tides at a given time anywhere in the world. This is not really too difficult, because we know the Moon and the Sun affect water through a gravitational pull. But scientists have learned that the causes of the north and south air mass movements, which cause the cool- and warm-weather waves, are north and south tangential "tidal thrusts" timed by the movements of the Moon. These tidal thrusts are the force that starts the air masses in motion. Because it is the orbit of the Moon that causes the tides, astronomical mathematics can calculate these movements for every day a year in advance.

Such a systematic method of measurement forms the basis of Selby Maxwell's forecasting system, but his greatest contribution was to delineate the correct time lags that cause the turbulent upper air masses to act in the predetermined manner which they do.

Maxwell thought that if north and south tangential tidal thrusts were strong enough to vary the tides, they might also initiate the movement of air masses. When the daily location of these tidal thrusts were plotted, they revealed close correlation with the daily location and movements of the air masses as shown on Weather Bureau observation maps. He learned how to plot the air masses over land masses. Maxwell claimed that this is the key to predicting the weather.

Air tides are influenced by the Moon in much the same way the sea tides are. In essence, the jet stream in our upper atmosphere is equivalent to another Moon. The jet stream travels at velocities up to six hundred miles per hour, faster from west to east than the Earth is turning at the equator. Hence, these air tides are in orbit, and the orbit of one affects the orbit of the other.

Maxwell developed his formula of weather prediction by being able to chart the movement of the jet stream by the motion and declination of the Moon.

The proper determination of *Time,* rather than *position,* of Earth, Moon, Sun and upper air masses, led to Maxwell's perfecting the formula that has permitted researchers to accumulate a thirty-year record of accurate weather forecasts made one to five years in advance. The center of the jet stream is always where the storm activity is. It comes down during the warmer seasons and it shifts back up during the winter months because of the inclination of Earth. But the jet stream is in free orbit. And we know the cycles because we know the tides of the jet stream. This makes it possible for us to predict major storms, not just three or four days in advance, but three or four years in advance. Using Maxwell's research, we can predict the movement of air currents as accurately as science can predict the height of tides.

3

A Psychology of World Climate

Raymond Wheeler first became interested in world climate because of a problem he encountered while teaching the history of psychology at the University of Kansas. In his own words:

"Since 1912, developments in psychology have proceeded along two theoretically opposite and incompatible lines. On the one hand there have been behaviorism and conditioned response psychology that have followed the strictly orthodox, mechanistic principles of association. These psychologies assumed that human behavior, regarded either subjectively or objectively, was a complex pattern of phenomena built up by bond-forming processes from simple elemental responses, in such a way that, piece by piece, the resulting pattern of the whole was obtained mechanically from preexisting parts. The basic fact was the simple experience. Mind was passive.

"Opposed to this view there sprang up several varieties of gestalt or organic psychology, whose common thesis is that behavior, from the beginning, is an already integrated pattern of responses, however simple: that complexity is achieved not by the procedure of obtaining wholes from parts, but of parts from wholes, through processes known as expansion and individuation (differentiation). The basic fact is the whole mind, the personality. Mind is active."

Wheeler's extended review of history yielded a surprise: Periods in which mechanistic behaviorism was generally accepted tended to alternate with periods in which the organic point of view was in vogue.

Extending the inquiry further, Wheeler brought to light alternations in an entire culture pattern; the components of which were merely parts of an integrated, fluctuating whole.

This fluctuating culture pattern turned out to be synchronized with the rise and fall of governments, nations and empires—the organic expression coinciding with the rise of strong states and totalitarianism; the mechanistic with the weakening or fall of militaristic governments and the growth of democratic institutions.

This shifting back and forth carried with it reversals in attitude, feeling, judgment, purpose, and degrees of tolerance and intolerance, to such an extent that human lives, on a wholesale basis, were free or not, hurled into war or not, in accordance with these fluctuations. The norms of acceptable and unacceptable behavior were widely affected by these variances in attitudes. The former were closely associated with organic, absolutist and totalitarian cultures, while the latter were associated with atomistic, mechanistic, utilitarian and democratic cultures.

One evening, Raymond Wheeler presented these facts to a group of scientists. During the discussion that followed, a member of the group inquired if the cultural fluctuations had been compared with the tree-growth curve obtained by measuring the annual growth rings of the 3,300-year-old California sequoias.

"The question was at first puzzling," Wheeler confesses in his journals, "for what possible relationship could there be between. . .cultural fluctuations in human society and. . .fluctuations in the rate of growth of the big trees in California? At any rate, the inquirer who had recently seen the sequoia curve thought he recognized a similarity between it and the culture curve, which had just been presented."

In those geographical localities where seasons are regular and stable, trees lay down one layer of light cells during the winter. An expert can measure these rings and plot the measurements in the form of a curve.

The widest rings are laid down during the longest growing seasons; i.e., during those years in which there are long seasons favorable for rapid growth. It turns out that these are the years when the weather trend in the vicinity where the trees are located was warm and wet. In a warm year the growing season is longer. Warmth, moisture, and the long growing season, all taken together, produce the widest rings.

On the other hand, a narrow ring is produced either by a very dry or short growing season or a combination of the two. It so happens that the longest periods when the trees were growing slowly were also times when the years were both cold and dry, when the winters were long and rainfall poor throughout the year.

"Studies show that the sequoia tree-ring curves indicate what the world weather trends were like much of the time down through history," Wheeler wrote.

"The peaks and troughs of . . . the sequoia curve and the culture curve corresponded so well down through the centuries that . . . laws of chance could not account for the similarity. There seemed to be only one plausible explanation, namely, that . . . fluctuations in . human behavior were associated with fluctuations in world weather trends, or climatic fluctuations. In other words. . . this led to the suspicion that man's behavior might possibly be conditioned by climate in a way hitherto unsuspected.

"The next questions were: Did the fluctuations in tree growth adequately reflect the weather trends? Were these weather trends really worldwide in scope? Accordingly, an intensive study of human behavior in relation to climatic changes was then begun.

"From there on evidence was collected as rapidly as possible. . ."

Tree-ring curves are only one of many sources of information that Wheeler used to check his history of world weather. Among other areas of research were the following:

• Chronologies kept by various governments, army headquarters, monasteries or other interested organizations or individuals, containing items about the weather such as droughts, heat waves, cold waves, excessive rain, floods, storms, excessive snow, famines, crop failures, locust plagues, forest fires, freezing and thawing dates, harvesting dates, lake and river levels, glacial retreats and advances, travel in the mountains (passes open for lack of snow or passes closed by excessive snow), the freezing over of large bodies of water, the freezing over of the Baltic Sea between Germany and Scandinavia, the blocking of coastal commerce by excessive ice and so on.

• Lake and river levels as determined by geographical and geological analyses. These include the location and dating of old beaches on hillsides and buildings now under water.

• Reports of sunspots large enough to be seen with the naked eye. When a group of large sunspots is seen, it is certain to turn cold for a period of years soon thereafter. Large spots are likely to recur during long cold periods. Warm periods are noted for their absence of large spots.

• Pollen analysis of successive layers of the soil, indicating a series of changes in various forests.

In addition, a study of history shows a number of civilizations that held their own beliefs regarding the cyclical nature of time. Ancient Hindu literature is full of references to the supposed rise and fall of cultural cycles. Babylonian and Chinese literature contains similar references. The ancient

Greeks held to a rhythmic conception of history, and they were also conscious of a possible relationship between historical events and climate.

Cyclic theories of history were popular during certain periods in the Middle Ages, in the sixteenth and seventeenth centuries, and again during the early nineteenth. Geographer Ellsworth Huntington correlated the rise and fall of civilizations with climatic changes.

Huntington believed that history is, in part, determined by the simple process of climatic change from warm to cold and wet to dry, and also by the degree to which the environment is climatically stimulating. According to Huntington, the ancient civilizations were in the southern part of the temperate zone because the Earth was cooler then. Northern Europe and central Asia were too cold, probably too dry, when Greece had its glory and Rome had its grandeur. Huntington's work maintains that the main storm tracks of the north temperate zone were farther south than they are now. When they moved north, with an expansion of the temperate zone, civilization moved north with them.

During the twentieth century, along with a great interest in patterns of human behavior, emphasis is again on establishing a relationship between weather-energy cycles and all phases of human activity.

However, a study of the literature on periodicities in rainfall, temperature, tree growth, volume of business, and so forth, can certainly leave you confused. And some of the historical works on alleged secular cycles and recurrent periods of activity simply cannot survive critical analysis. So it is with certain studies that purport to have found definite secular periods in which climatic and historical events repeat themselves in synchronized fashion.

Any effort to visualize the history of climate solely in terms of single, secular periods—or to regard cultural cycles in the same manner— hopelessly oversimplifies the case.

Wheeler and Maxwell began their research to gather all the facts. Their opinions and conclusions were not preconceived. The facts were not studied to prove a point. Their research was begun for the purpose of learning why there were complete reversals in viewpoints, in governments, in the sciences and in basic human affairs during specific periods of time. Their research was begun to build curves of those trends in human affairs.

It was only later, when these trends were compared to the curves of the weather trends and cycles, that the correlation was discovered.

Only after the trends and cycles in human affairs were found to be in direct correlation with the changes and trends in the weather was the research actually begun to collect all of the facts in relation to both. The purpose was to learn if the correlation would continue *after* all of the facts were assembled.

Twenty thousand pieces of art were studied. Literature throughout history was analyzed. More than eighteen thousand battles and military campaigns were studied, and the facts collected and assembled in relation to their timing.

Moreover, Maxwell and Wheeler did not list historical data from only a few parts of the world. They ploughed through thousands of volumes of history relating to every known nation that ever existed. The Orient as well as the Western world was carefully analyzed. Every phase of the Maxwell-Wheeler research was done with extreme thoroughness.

4

The One-Hundred-Year Cycle

Maxwell and Wheeler ran into an important one-hundred-year period, both in the historic and climatic cycles. Wheeler writes: "Tree rings in sufficient quantity locate the majority of the warm and cold and wet and dry phases of the one-hundred-year cycles in the weather trends; the weather trends themselves are generally worldwide in scope."

Wheeler summarized all of the climatic evidence in the form of a climate curve, showing the position of the phases of the one-hundred-year cycle with its interruptions. This curve was then compared with the succession of cultural events. It was evident that the climatic and cultural fluctuations had occurred together down through history. Either the cultural cycles were conditioned by the climatic cycles, or both were the results of the same unknown cause.

A study of available temperature and rainfall records pointed out that this worldwide one-hundred-year weather trend, or climatic cycle, passes through a definite succession of stages, repeated in the same order as the cycle repeats. Additional evidence confirmed the existence of this cycle. In fact, Wheeler found it is possible to trace it back at least to 600 B.C.

These are not mechanically or mathematically precise periods. Sometimes that longtime weather trend may shrink or expand a bit. But Maxwell and Wheeler found that it averages one hundred years in length and that it has a definite pattern that tends to repeat itself.

The cycle visible in the sequoia tree-ring curve is not always one hundred years in length. It shrinks at times to seventy years and lengthens at times to one hundred twenty years. It is usually either ninety or one hundred ten years long.

Dr. Wheeler was able to define that this very distinct one-hundred-year world weather rhythm, or cycle, was made up of four basic phases — warm-wet, followed by warm-dry, then by cold-wet, then by cold-dry.

And indeed, rainfall and temperature measurements for the last two hundred years also point to rhythms within rhythms, or cycles within cycles. The warm half of the one-hundred-year cycle, approximately fifty years in length, is interrupted every so often by temporary drops in temperature. Usually these drops in temperature occur every 11.2 years, when sunspot activity is greatest. Sometimes the interruption will last for only a year or so, sometimes for ten years.

The cold half of the one-hundred-year cycle undergoes corresponding interruptions. Every so often, temperatures rise for a year or two, or up to a period of ten years. Usually this temperature rise centers around a period of minimal sunspot activity.

The wettest times on the climatic cycle occur during transitions from the long cold phase to the warm phase and back again. The same type of event occurs in the annual weather cycle of the seasons.

Over large areas of Earth, the wettest times of the year are the spring and fall, as it is turning warm or cold. In fact, the annual cycle reveals the same successive phases as does the long one-hundred-year cycle, namely, a cold-dry mid or late summer, a cold-wet fall and early winter, then a cold-dry mid or late winter again.

It happens, therefore, that the first part of the warm phase of the one-hundred-year cycle is the wettest (this is the warm-wet phase) and the last part is the driest (the warm-dry phase).

Similarly, the first part of the cold phase of the one-hundred-year cycle is the wettest (the cold-wet phase) and the last part is the driest (the cold-dry phase).

Temperatures reach their highest point in the one-hundred-year cycle during the warm-dry phase and their lowest point during the cold-dry phase. In other words, temperatures are most moderate during periods of normal or abundant rainfall.

Of course, even though the culture "cycles" corresponded with the California sequoia curve in a manner that could not be accounted for by chance, this does not mean that the weather trend in California is always a true indication of world weather, nor does it mean that every part of the world is experiencing the same type of weather trend at exactly the same time. There are always areas in which the weather temporarily runs contrary to the world trend at a particular time. There are also areas that are slowly becoming drier over long periods of time, or gradually wetter.

Even in these areas, however, the general pattern of worldwide fluctuations is still discernible.

Ever since Maxwell and Wheeler began making long-range weather predictions on the basis of predictable successions of changes in the Earth's atmosphere, skeptics have maintained that different parts of the world have separate and unrelated climates. World weather, the doubters have insisted, simply cannot be demonstrated.

The evidence gathered by Maxwell and Wheeler demonstrates that world weather is one very complex, but nevertheless single, phenomenon. World weather constitutes a single whole, in which every part is related to every other. In order to understand the rain that is falling in one's backyard, it is necessary to know the principles of world weather.

"The first and foremost principle of world weather is *diversity within a unit,*" Raymond Wheeler often stated.

The causes of world weather are numerous and complex, but of two general kinds. One set causes unity and uniformity in world weather. These are two quite different things. Weather can be quite different in various places and yet be unified. Another set of causes produces diversity; that is, different kinds of weather at the same time in different parts of the world.

"In other words," Wheeler explained, "as different as temperature or rainfall may be in different parts of the world (diversity), these differences are only specialized parts of a unified whole. All the different parts share in the properties of the whole, just as the brain, stomach and liver, although different, share in the life of the whole body."

Wheeler's accumulation of materials concerning the history of world weather includes the following data:

• When reports of extreme cold, excessive snow, and freezing and thawing dates are collected from all the known parts of the earth, they cluster in the same decades of history. It is the same with reports of excessive heat, rain, storms and droughts.

•Heat waves, cold waves, sudden increases or decreases in rainfall — even of two to five years' duration — occur repeatedly over many widely separated areas.

• Large masses of data show that periods of minimal sunspot activity tend to be warmer and drier over most of the known areas of the world. Periods of intense sunspot activity are colder and drier.

• Masses of data indicate that down through history the warm and cold decades have been so widespread as to be practically universal the world over.

These same masses of data show that the four main climatic phases of the one-hundred-year cycle, disturbed only by secondary leads and lags, occur simultaneously. However, if they are in cycles as short as ten years or less, these phases may not always occur simultaneously. One continent or part of a continent will lead or lag behind another.

The shift from the warm to the cold phase of the one-hundred-year cycle, or from the cold phase to the warm phase, does not occur exactly at the same time over all parts of Earth. Nor will it be equally warm or equally cold each year in countries located at the same distance from the equator.

It is the same with rainfall. One part of the world may lead or lag as much as twenty years behind another in reaching the warm side of the average or the cold side of the average, yet discrepancies are the exception rather than the rule.

But over a period of years, the great waves of coldness, heat, rain or dryness will have covered most of the large continental areas, affecting most, if not all, of the longtime averages in much the same way. The majority of the areas will participate sooner or later in the same world trends.

Even when one part of the world is losing or gaining rainfall much faster than another area (i.e., when a local trend varies from the world trend), world trends and cycles of other lengths still show on top of the varying secular trend.

The extent of the fluctuations in temperature and rainfall during the longtime changes in weather trends depends upon the location of the area in question. The warmer countries do not fluctuate to the same extent as do the cooler countries (the tropics least of all); yet they fluctuate approximately at the same time.

World weather trends are most uniform during the height of the warm-wet and cold-dry phases of the one-hundred-year cycle, and least uniform during the transitions from the cold to the warm side, or vice versa. During and right after these transitions, the world as a whole receives its maximum rainfall and is, therefore, the most stormy.

"The climate curve is intended to represent – as far as one curve can – the weather trend in the world as a whole at any one time," Wheeler explained.

"The curve has no absolute significance. The meaning of the curve at any one point is relative to the pattern of the one-hundred-year cycle as a whole."

Dr. Raymond Wheeler's extended inquiry showed that all weather fluctuations paralleled a broad, universal culture pattern that, in spite of its vast intricacy, was alternating back and forth as a single unit. Alternations between the mechanistic and wholistic patterns that Wheeler had first started speculating about seemed to cover all human activity at any time in history and anywhere on Earth.

History was found to consist of alternating mechanistic and wholistic times or periods. A complete fluctuation in the order of a cycle averaged almost exactly one hundred years in length, although it varied considerably from a minimum of about seventy years to a maximum of about one hundred twenty years. The majority of the fluctuations were either ninety or one hundred ten years long.

Dr. Wheeler found that during the mechanistic half of the cycle, the emphasis in human activity and thought everywhere was on the part of anything rather than on the whole – often at the expense of the whole.

In science the emphasis was on the atom; in biology, on the individual organ or the cell; in mathematics, on the infinitesimal, or the individual number.

In politics it was on the individual rights as opposed to the state, and on a laissez-faire attitude to regulation rather than on socialism.

In psychology it was on the individual "faculty" of the mind – that is, the individual experience or individual response – rather than on the mind or personality as a whole. In art it was on detail rather than on the overall composition.

During mechanistic times art has always been dominated by highly decorative styles like the baroque and rococo. In dress the ornate Elizabethan and Victorian types of costume prevailed.

The mechanistic point of view has always generated a respect for minuteness of detail, accuracy of measurement and great collections and classifications of descriptive facts. The painstaking collecting by the famous pioneer botanist Carolus Linnaeus in the eighteenth century and the work of Charles Darwin in the nineteenth century are typical examples of mechanistic achievements.

On the other hand, the mechanistic pattern has never led to a profound understanding of nature.

During mechanistic times, causation is sought in the "mechanical" operation of the brain; but during wholistic times, causation is sought within the mind itself, as opposed to the brain.

In turn, this emphasis has led to the stressing of dreams, as in the case of Freudian psychology.

The wholistic pattern has led to theories of the mind as a whole and to a study of the personality of the whole person and his or her adjustment to the world. Since this world is largely a social one from the standpoint of human problems, the wholistic trend has always stressed social behavior and adjustment. Theories of the subconscious have been popular.

During the wholistic periods the emphasis everywhere was on the whole rather than on the part – often at the expense of the part.

These were the periods in the history of science when basic laws were sought pertaining to the operation of the universe in general, such as the law of gravity in the days of Galileo and later the laws of motion of Newton, the gas laws of Boyle, the laws of electricity and thermodynamics in the early nineteenth century, and now the generalized principles of relativity and of quantum and wave mechanics. Basic laws of nature have always been investigated by the wholistic, rather than by the mechanistic, pattern of scientific thinking.

In the arts, the emphasis on the whole as opposed to the parts has always led to abstract movements – a streamlining of styles – and eventually to some form of impressionism and the caricaturizing of themes. Modernism – the streamlining in architectural design, Impressionism and Cubism in painting and sculpture, and resorting to fantasies and subjectivism – are examples of the wholistic trend of art. Corresponding trends go back to the days of the caveman.

During the wholistic periods of history when philosophical and scientific minds were thinking in terms of basic universal interrelations, new nations and governments were being formed. People were becoming more unified, and new governments under strong rulers were becoming imperialistic.

In economic thinking the trend during wholistic periods is toward a "statism" of some kind, either under the rule of an absolute monarch or dictator or under a welfare, socialistic state. "Statism" can be defined as any nation that puts the welfare of the nation or state before the welfare of the individual.

In politics the wholistic point of view has invariably generated too great an emphasis upon the state as opposed to the individual. Absolutisms, socialisms, communisms and eras of dictators have been the outgrowth of misapplications of the wholistic pattern.

Developments in the arts and sciences have also come in waves, recurring repeatedly with the cold and warm cycles.

Human energies increase during cool weather trends. Business booms come at the end of a cold cycle and the beginning of the warm-wet cycle which follows. All the waves of rapid advancement throughout history have come in the cool cycles, or as result of the cool cycles.

Human energies decrease during the warm cycles and bring decadence to human affairs.

Increased production resulting from improved growing conditions occurs during the warm-wet cycle.

Birthrates, however, decrease in warm times; and as the warm period advances, human energies are depleted even more. The effect of the lowered energy gradually produces an economic depression.

Wheeler's cycles would be of only modest use if they only correlated with changes of "mood" or taste. What is striking is that they can also pinpoint specific events.

Throughout history, dictators, tyrannies and the major wars between strong nations have come during each and every warm cycle.

Throughout history, civil wars and swings to democratic forms of government have repeatedly come on each cold cycle.

Wheeler found that the two kinds of wars alternated with one another; that is, there would be a time in history when international wars prevailed, then another when civil wars prevailed. If a war happened to be a mixture of the two, half of it was recorded as international, half as civil.

Entries or tallies were made of the number of international battles. These tallies were arranged above a midline, and the heights of these tallies were made proportional to the severity of the battles. Under the same plan, tallies for the civil war battles were arranged below a midline. In this way the positions of the peaks and the valleys were determined exactly by the dates of the battles fought in the wars.

In fact, Wheeler discovered that the dates of battles alone would have been sufficient to locate warm and cold periods of history with striking accuracy.

After a curve had been drawn, it was found that the peaks and the troughs based on the wars of history coincided in an astonishing manner with the peaks and troughs of the composite sequoia tree-ring curve taken from trees growing on the western slopes of the southern Sierra Nevada in California. In this region the seasons repeat themselves in such a regular manner that the sequoias almost always lay down one ring a year. These rings can be counted, and the age of the tree determined.

There are long periods of time when the average rings are relatively wide, and periods when they are relatively narrow. These periods alternate. The periods of wider rings are represented by peaks in the curve, and the periods of narrow rings by the troughs. These peaks and troughs coincide in a close manner with the peaks and troughs of the wars of history when they are divided into international and civil wars.

It has been shown that the longtime peaks of the sequoia curve occur during warm times and the troughs during cold times. The growing seasons are longer during warm years, hence the rings are wider. But the rings are also determined by the amount of rainfall. The rings are wide during wet years and narrow during dry years. They are the widest during periods in which there is a generous amount of warmth and moisture, narrowest when it is both cold and dry. The dating of the peaks and troughs of the economic-culture-climate curve was therefore determined jointly by the distribution of wars and by the dating of positions of the major peaks and troughs of the tree-ring curve.

In regard to temperature, the story as told by the trees in relation to known fluctuations in weather in recent centuries was applied to the earlier centuries and thoroughly checked against thousands of individual items found in various documents of the past. That is, actual weather events such as heat waves, cold waves, storms, blizzards; crop failures, famines, locust plagues, harvesting dates; dates when ice broke up or formed on lakes and rivers; lake and river levels; and so on.

It turned out that when international battles were plotted above a midline and civil war battles below, the resulting curve provided an excellent representation of the rise and fall of empires, nations and governments throughout history.

On the peak (or warm) side, where international wars prevail, empires are strong and unified and prosperous enough to wage these wars.

On the trough (or cold) side, where, along with anarchy, civil wars prevail, governments have collapsed. Factions among the people of different political or religious beliefs tear the country apart. (Out of this chaos, however, emerges a new national feeling in a new generation of people under fresh leadership. The movement accelerates as the cold period comes to an end and reaches a climax just as it is turning warm.)

When compared with curves of measured temperature and rainfall, their distribution showed that international wars were typically warm-phase events, while civil wars occurred most often during the cold phases. The curves showing the distribution of these battles over the centuries would have located the warm and cold periods of history for the world as a whole.

The famous civil wars of history have always occurred during the long cold periods: for example, the civil wars between the aristocratic and democratic parties in the Greek city-states, circa 400 B.C.; the civil wars between Caesar and Pompey, then between Anthony and Octavius in the 40s and 30s B.C.; the civil wars all over the world in the second half of the 400s A.D., typified by the official fall of Rome (and of all the other ancient empires as well).

In more modern times there have been the civil wars between the English houses of Lancaster and York in England (the Wars of the Roses), which occurred during the cold parts of the fifteenth century, and the fierce religious wars in Holland and France in the 1500s, which came during cold decades, as did the Reformation.

The American and French revolutions broke out at the end of a long cold period. The South American wars of independence fought under the leadership of Bolivar occurred during cold times, as did the American Civil War.

Because we have just ended a warm period and are well into a cold period, we are now beginning a period of potential civil wars.

The difference between "hot" international wars and "cold" civil wars makes better sense when we recall the natural progression from wholistic (hot) politics to mechanistic (cold) politics and back again. Whenever a wholistic political whole overemphasizes the state at the expense of the individual, there invariably develops a wave of socialistic and communistic theory, along with the emergence of tyrants, dictators, despots, police systems, reactionism and a contraction of all freedoms that had evolved up to that time in history.

With the growth of strong governments, there occurs an outburst of international wars. This occurs when the culture pattern is shifting as a whole from the piecemeal emphasis to an emphasis on wholes.

The outbreak of international "nation-building wars" are invariable symptoms of the revival of nation-building following a period of political (mechanistic) stagnation. Periods of nation-building, coinciding with the reappearance of the wholistic culture pattern as a whole, invariably end in periods of social, political and moral decline, and a period of universal despotism.

At this point in the cycle, nations are on the way to collapse, or at least governments are about to break down. As part of the breakdown process, another wave of international wars occurs, which are symptomatic of political decline or degeneracy, or at least of political extremism. These wars occur on the reverse transition; that is, as the wholistic shifts back to the mechanistic pattern. They give way to civil strife in the form of revolts, rebellions and other extreme movements.

People all over the world, whose suffering under an autocracy of one kind or another has reached a climax, then possess the initiative and determination to free themselves and to revive and extend the democratic institutions they had known previously, but which had nearly been lost during the trend toward statism. Several decades are then taken up with the process of emancipation. During the process of nation-building, a new aristocracy, or minority party of some kind, had seized power. This privileged class is then overthrown, and participation in the government is extended to a larger percentage of society. A new generation sets up a new, more democratic government – only to initiate another trend in the direction of absolutism and tyranny as the culture patterns shift once more from the mechanistic back to the wholistic emphasis.

Thus it is that the civil wars of history have been associated with the mechanistic pattern, and international wars with the wholistic.

5

The Five-Hundred-Year Cycle

As a result of his extensive research, Dr. Raymond Wheeler was able to chart five-hundred-year climatic cycles throughout history. Wheeler found that, both climatically and culturally, secondary climaxes of cold temperatures and devastating droughts, together with great waves of migrations and drastic revolutions in society, have occurred at the end of each intervening five-hundred-year period.

Every fifth cold phase is an unusually severe one, as demonstrated by the fifth century B.C. and the first, fifth, tenth, and fifteenth centuries A.D. Wheeler's research indicated that the sixth century B.C., the fifth century A.D., and the fifteenth century A.D. were also unusually cold and dry times. They were centuries of widespread migrations, periods of low lake-levels and slow tree-growth. All three were characterized by the same process – the death of an old world and the birth of a new one.

The main divisions of history – ancient, medieval and modern – serve also as landmarks in the history of world climate, Wheeler said. "Old civilizations collapse and new civilizations are born on tides of climatic change. The turning points occur when cold-dry times reach their maximum severity."

Every second termination of the five-hundred-year cycle naturally coincides with the termination of a thousand-year one. In the center of each thousand-year cycle there seems to be a much warmer period.

The first such period in our historical epoch reached a climax at the time of Julius and Augustus Caesar, about 40 B.C.; the second, around A.D. 900 and 1000. During the second of these warmer periods, Greenland and Iceland were colonized. Once the warm phase of the long cycle was on its way, Greenland froze up and has remained so ever since. Many times in the fourteenth and fifteenth centuries, the Baltic Sea froze over between Germany and Sweden, permitting horses, even armies, to cross from one country to another on the ice.

Every alternate five-hundred-year cycle has ended in the middle of the thousand-year rhythm during its warm phase. However, it seems as if there have always been complications:

The five-hundred-year cycle breaks down into shorter periods that, as we have seen, last about one hundred years on the average. These clearly defined cycles each have a major warm phase and a major cold phase, two major wet and two major dry periods. (One major wet period occurs at the beginning of the warm phase, the other at the beginning of the cold phase. One major dry period occurs at the end of the warm phase, the other at the end of the cold phase.)

Raymond Wheeler believed that each great revolution of history, synchronous with the termination of a five-hundred-year cycle, has been characterized by a great advance in democratic benefits to the common people.

The year 575 B.C. marked the termination of both a five-hundred-year and a thousand-year cycle. Up to that time, the inhabitants of Europe were largely still Stone Age nomads. Little enlightened thought had yet existed anywhere in the world, with the exception of rudimentary engineering, metallurgy and agriculture in Egypt. China and the older civilizations of Mesopotamia had fallen into decline. The last strong power to assert itself had been Assyria, and its final brilliance had already run its course. The older of the ancient empires, with their god-kings, were gone forever, together with the great tombs, temples and religions that had sustained them.

The beginning of the mental attitude and intelligence that would produce modern civilization began in 575 B.C. Primitive techniques of structuring mental processes gave way to such Greek philosophers and scientists as Thales and Pythagoras, who prepared the intellectual climate for Plato, Aristotle, Euclid and Archimedes.

This was the beginning of scientific knowledge; the beginning of a rational search for truth; the beginning of mathematics and logic; the beginning of serious analyses of social, political and ethical problems; and it was the beginning of democracy as we know it. There was also an industrial revolution, the emergence of new crafts, enlarged perimeters of trade areas.

During this five-hundred-year cycle, the centers of civilization shifted from south and east of the Mediterranean to the peninsulas on the north. This period was dominated by Greece, Macedonia and Rome, with Persia steadily offering competition. The Greek city-states, such as Athens and Sparta, had their Golden Ages. The cycle which began in 575 B.C. saw the growth of Greek democracy, emerging from the convulsions of the sixth century B.C.

As the city-states declined, Rome gained in power. Rome's greatest contribution came from her genius for law and organization, but she had reached the climax of her power just before the five-hundred-year cycle drew to a close.

The next five-hundred-year cycle of our historical epoch ended at the time Jesus Christ was born. Until A.D. 70, much of the first century was cold. The great Roman Empire, which had taken five hundred years to build, has passed her cultural prime and was beginning to sink.

Although the second five-hundred-year cycle saw the emergence of no great powers in the West, the life and teachings of Jesus had begun another kind of revolution and transformation.

During the next cycle, while the Roman Empire was crumbling, the spread of Christianity emphasized the importance of the individual life and conscience and universal concern for all humanity. The Roman Empire struggled for its very existence during this period, and the ever-shrinking boundaries of its once far-reaching domain dissolved to memories when the cycle ended.

Asia was the center of political energy in the world during the second five-hundred-year cycle.

The two major events of the West were the rise of the papacy in Rome and Constantine's adoption of Christianity as the state religion. It was Constantine, ruling from Constantinople, who carved out the later Byzantine Empire.

Our historical epoch has not known a time of greater migrations than those that occurred in the fourth and fifth centuries at the end of the second five-hundred-year cycle. A severe deterioration of world climate, climaxed by long droughts, thoroughly dried out the uplands of Asia. Following this, the civilizations of the northern Mediterranean shores soon felt the force of the mighty Asiatic hordes.

The year 575 B.C. had centered in a cold-dry period that lasted for about one hundred years.

The cold-dry period that began about the time of Christ's birth lasted for seventy-five years.

The immediate cold period surrounding A.D. 460 lasted for only about thirty years; but for a considerable period of time before and after 460, the warm phases were very short and were interrupted by unusually long successions of cold years with abnormally low rainfall.

Long cold periods are always characterized by revolutions, civil wars and weak governments. Often, during the cold periods, there may be no government at all in large areas of the world.

So it was in A.D. 560 that empires all over the world collapsed; trade routes were abandoned; learning declined; darkness descended upon the beacon lights of civilization.

In the fifth century slavery as it was known and practiced by the ancient world came to an end and was replaced by serfdom. Although serfdom in one sense was only another form of slavery, it permitted numerous freedoms which the old forms of forced servitude did not include.

When the Roman Empire collapsed altogether, cultural initiative shifted from the West to the East. The old culture died painfully at the end of a thousand-year cycle.

The rebuilding in the third five-hundred-year cycle of our epoch was slow and the emergence from the Dark Ages difficult. The first great efforts were realized in the founding of the Greek Empire at Constantinople by Justinian and the simultaneous rebirth of Persia. In the latter part of the eighth century, Charlemagne unified the Franks and created the mighty state that would one day be France, but the West lay dormant during this cycle.

While a Dark Age engulfed most of Europe, Turks, Tartars and Huns built one large empire after another in Asia.

As part of the awakening in the world as a whole, Mohammed in 622 founded another of the world's great religions. Under the impetus of this new force, the Arabs began to extend their borders far to the East and to the West. With little resistance, they marched across North Africa. They claimed Spain, and had it not been for the strength of the Franks, they could have overrun all of western Europe.

Meanwhile, Baghdad was harboring a Golden Age of Arabian civilization that preserved the knowledge of the ancient Greeks for the world. But by the ninth century, both empires were in a state of decay.

The onset of long cold-dry periods once again brought about civil wars and migrations. Asia declined in political initiative, but not in cultural innovation. Justinian and the great Byzantine Empire, together with the vital Arabian civilization that migrated from North Africa into Spain, built a new West. At the same time, China and Japan underwent an important cultural renaissance. Baghdad entered a Golden Age. Charlemagne carved out a dynamic kingdom in Europe. But the close of the five-hundred-year cycle saw all of these civilizations in decline. In the ninth and tenth centuries great storms and bitter cold devastated Asia, driving hordes of Norsemen out of Scandinavia until they had overrun Europe down to the tip of southern Italy and had conquered England.

With the ending of the medieval age, the culture of Asia once more declined, and the five-hundred-year cycle that would belong to Europe brought with it the Renaissance. The new world, which had been born out of the furious civil wars and the invasions of migrating hordes, witnessed the following great events of the fourth five-hundred-year cycle:

• England was invaded and settled by the Saxons, Scandinavians and Normans.

• The various tribal cultures of Europe accepted Christianity, built cities, accumulated wealth and laid the foundations for the principalities that were to become Europe's modern nations.

• Christian principalities took root in northern Spain.

• The agency of the Christian Church unified Europe.

• The revolution that began in the tenth century brought into being the modern merchant class and eventually the free, and democratic, city-state. The merchant class instituted the principle of justice to supplement the principle of loyalty in the feudal world. The merchants also did a great deal to demand the inception of constitutional government.

• Crusades were carried out against the Seljuk Turks.

• There was a great revival of learning and the creation of large universities with the rediscovery of ancient Greek culture. Commerce revived and great banking systems emerged. Feudalism developed with its own economic and political pattern.

• The Holy Roman Empire was founded. In Asia there emerged the extraordinary Mongolian empire of Genghis Khan, which stretched from the China Sea to the borders of Europe, and which was later revived in eastern Asia by his grandson, Kubla Khan. At the close of the five-hundred-year cycle, Tamerlane would restore the great empire in western Asia. Elaborate civilizations developed in Indochina, in Central America and in the mountains of Peru.

Although the accomplishments achieved during the fourth five-hundred-year cycle were many, by the time it drew to a close, the peasant classes had begun to revolt against both the authority of the church and their feudal lords. In turn, the kings and princes were warring with the popes and the church for secular power and freedom of action.

Intellectual and religious freedoms grew in spite of the inquisition. These prepared the way for modern constitutional governments, in spite of the temporary power of the principle of the divine right of kings. Intellectual freedom made naturalistic, modern science possible and increased the scope and opportunities for self-expression by demanding communication through nationalistic tongues, instead of Latin.

A new and free merchant class had come into being, and banking systems were encouraging an industrial, as well as a cultural, revolution.

The great Asiatic empires had collapsed. The magnificent cities of Indochina and the empire of the Maya in Central America succumbed to the ravages of an encroaching jungle. The kingdom of the Peruvian Incas sunk into decline.

As one-hundred-year, five-hundred-year, and thousand-year cycles all ended at the same time, the old world died in a cataclysm.

As part of the new awakening, the Renaissance burst forth. For the first time in our historical epoch, large numbers of people began to express themselves in art, in literatures of their native tongues, in bold explorations to faraway places. New universities sprang up in an intellectual climate much more conducive to free expression.

The Reformation, with its emphasis on religious freedom, gave vital impetus to the onward march of democracy. The dawn of modern science established a social revolution based on the substitution of natural for divine laws. The invention of movable type printing only stimulated these many revolutions.

As the weather during the one-thousand-year cycle became warmer, the great centers of progress moved north, where they have remained to the present day.

The 100-Year Climatic and Culture Cycles of History

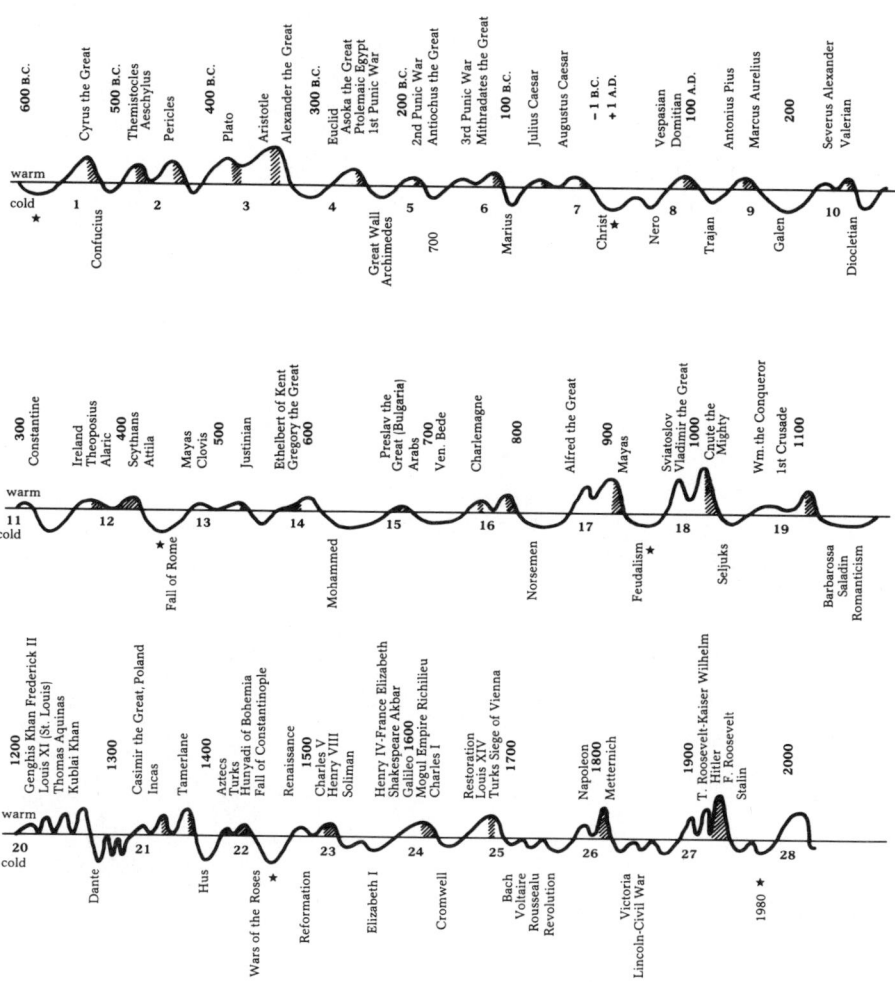

★ = 500-Year Cycle

6

The Cycles of Time and Human Ecology

Is our behavior really linked to humidity and temperature? If environment is a strong enough factor to condition the structural features of a plant or an animal, how much more must it determine directly and indirectly the behavior of the nervous system, the habits, temperament, attitudes, tolerances and intolerances, intelligence, and even the thoughts and the aesthetic life of human beings?

"The climates of the different areas of Earth produce different kinds of plants and animals," Wheeler observed. "No one disputes this fact. Their physical characteristics, their habits, and their behavior are determined in large measures by the climate in which they live. When the climate changes, the plants and animals must adjust or die. Dramatic changes in the climate are what has caused so many species to disappear from Earth in the past.

"Man is as much a part of the life of Earth as are plants, crops and animals. One would not expect man to be immune to the conditions that affect and influence plants and animals, and he most definitely is not."

Temperatures do have a direct influence upon the physiology of the body.

The human body is like an engine that must convert one form of energy to another. In doing so, like any other engine, it creates heat. The body must get rid of this heat. Ordinarily it does so by radiation. However, when outside temperatures are high, radiation is often too slow. Unless the entire body is slowed down and generates less heat, fever and death will result.

When temperatures are high, the body tissues swell and contain more water. The blood vessels open up to help the escape of heat; the blood turns acidic; blood pressure falls; breathing is more shallow; the body receives less oxygen and loses weight. The nerve reactions are speeded up.

If the body stays hot enough, it has to remain at a low level of activity. There is no reserve energy for extra accomplishments or hard work. Growth slows down; the body is less resistant to disease; progress is slow; fertility low. Action must be less vigorous. More time must be spent resting.

Dr. William F. Petersen, a pioneer investigator of the influences of weather on various diseases, was interested primarily in the medical side of climatology. According to his observations, there is a tendency for introverted personalities to prefer warm weather and for extroverted personalities to prefer cold weather.

Introverts, whose minds turn inward, are concerned with thinking and imagination, sympathy, and the importance of security. They are less happy and stable during cold times and are tense and unstable during cold waves.

Introverts like warm weather, and they stabilize on rising temperatures (until it gets too hot).

Extroverts, whose minds turn outward, are concerned with action, competition, practicality and freedom. They are less happy and stable during warm times and are tense and unstable during heat waves. They like cold weather and are most stable during falling temperatures (until it gets too cold). Weather that makes the strong stronger makes the weak weaker.

In cold weather or in cool climates, blood pressure is higher; hearts beat faster; glands are more active; in general, metabolism and growth are faster. The blood vessels constrict to save heat; fat develops in the interest of conserving body heat against cold outside temperatures; and animals and human beings alike are more alert, aggressive, stable, tolerant and intelligent. The same conditions that produce action produce higher IQs, more competitive spirit, faster technological progress and greater tolerance.

Salespeople who make their calls after a storm when it is cool and the barometer is rising will find the buyer more receptive and more tolerant. On cool and stormy days more people get to work on time, and there are not as many absences.

But it must not get too cold. Cool weather and cool climate have their disadvantages. Ulcers are likely to act up or perhaps the appendix or even the gall bladder. When it gets too cold, humans become less stable.

Dr. Wheeler went on to illustrate that experiments on animals show that there is an optimum temperature for the development of size, stability of behavior, fertility and intelligence.

According to the research data of Dr. Ellsworth Huntington, there is also a best temperature for human intelligence and vitality.

In a study made of the efficiency of factory workers in Denmark, Japan, Pennsylvania, New York, Maryland, the Carolinas, Georgia and Florida, it was found that there was a pronounced peak of physical activity in the spring and fall, with valleys in midwinter and midsummer. Corresponding variations were found in mental output.

The mathematics grades of West Point Cadets, the percentage of individuals passing civil service examinations, the scores of students taking college entrance exams – all show spring and fall highs, midsummer and midwinter lows.

Huntington looked at these results and believed that they showed optimum temperatures for physical and mental activity. He set them at 38°F for mental work, 68° to 70°F for physical activity.

For the "best" effects there must be a moderately large difference between summer and winter temperatures and between night and day temperatures. An active, competitive civilization cannot thrive where it is warm the year around, where the nights are about as warm as the days, or where rainfall is not properly distributed throughout the year.

Only a relatively small land area of Earth has the kind of climate that is best-suited for human progress and technological advancement.

Parts of the Earth where these conditions are fulfilled to the greatest extent are the parts occupied by the highest levels of civilization, as measured in terms of scientific and technological progress and in standards of living. Today the optimum temperature belt for maximum human vigor runs through Western Europe – east to the Ural Mountains and the Black Sea – and Great Britain; across the Atlantic to southern Canada; the northern United States from New England through the Great Lakes region; and the southern United States during cold periods; the Northwest; then to Japan.

With some qualifications, the "optimum" area extends eastward across the Balkans and southern Russia as far as the Black Sea, and to a lesser extent, a portion of central China, parts of Korea and Manchuria; northern Argentina and central Chile; the southeastern part and southern tip of Africa; the southeastern corner of Australia and New Zealand.

Apparently the best climate for the whole variety of human endeavors ranges from 47° to 52° mean annual temperature, but 40° to 60°F is good. Very much beyond this range and it becomes either too cold or too hot for human vitality, intelligence, initiative and progress.

After the Ice Age, when the temperate zone expanded, the southern half became too warm – some areas too dry, other areas too wet – for maximum human vigor. This is now the condition across the

Mediterranean, Asia Minor, India, southern China and Central America — the very places where high civilizations once existed.

North Africa and Turkey have declined because it has been too warm and dry in those regions for several centuries. On the other hand, Great Britain became a great empire because the climate of the British Isles is about as good as any in the world for a steady maintenance of aggressiveness and vitality.

Germany became a powerful nation because of a stimulating climate, while Poland and Russia are most of the time too cold. China has never been able to unify because of her variety of climates.

It should be pointed out that one has to be very careful when speaking of the population of one climate being more vigorous than that of another. It has nothing to do with peoples or with ethnic groups; it has to do with climate, temperature, and weather-energy cycles!

Dr. Wheeler explained that the human organism must be very delicately adjusted to the prevailing temperatures of a given region. The delicacy of this adjustment is all the more remarkable in light of the fact that people living in the same country, under annual temperatures, say, of 46°F, as in Minnesota, carry on in the same political union in relative harmony with people living under annual temperatures of 66°F, as in Louisiana — a 20° difference. In both groups, we can expect attitudes of mind, tolerances and intolerances to change along the same lines, but to greater or lesser degrees as the temperature changes slightly in each region. Should a person move from one region to another, they will adjust, if they remain in the area long enough.

In any known region of the Earth, the most extreme difference in measured annual temperature between the coldest half-decade and warmest half-decade, up to 1930, does not exceed 6°. Most of the differences are considerably less than that. But a shift in annual temperatures of that amount may be the equivalent of a relocation to a considerably warmer environment.

A difference of 3°, in any region near the middle of the temperate zone, is going to change the relative length of summer and winter considerably. During cold years, which are often dry, the summers may be hot, although shorter, so that the differential applies mostly to the winter months. Hence the effect on human attitudes might be all the greater.

"To be sure, there was a time when cultural differences between the North and the South in the United States, obviously conditioned by climate, were the cause of a bloody civil war, for slave civilizations have never flourished well in cold regions, or in warmer regions during long cold periods," Dr. Wheeler admits.

"The difference of 3° and less, almost shockingly small, was probably much greater during earlier centuries of history when, perhaps, the warm phases were warmer and the cold phases colder than now. Nevertheless, a difference in mean annual temperature of no greater than 1½°F, when prevailing consistently for no longer than half a decade, is sufficient, anywhere on Earth, to start changes in the human behavior pattern in one direction or the other."

Dr. Wheeler's research data showed that it made no difference whether human beings lived in colder or warmer countries, in the Occident or the Orient. Their political behavior shifted in the same direction with the same shift in world climate. This was true regardless of the level of culture, or the degree to which the political unit in question was more or less democratic or totalitarian than another political unit.

"It seems likely that the difference in temperature alone will not account for the differences in human mental attitudes," Dr. Wheeler notes, "but that other climatic events which accompany rising and falling annual temperatures are important. . . . Storminess was associated, over the world as a whole, with climatic change, and when temperature had stabilized at an extreme level on either side of the axis, it was dry – that is, storms were much less frequent."

Under storms, of course, may be included ordinary rains. Thus, variability of the weather and, with longer periods of time, variability of climate go with temperatures that approach the longtime mean. The more invigorating and changeable climate (as to both temperature and storminess) occurs while annual temperatures prevail near average for a given region – that is, are near the average temperatures to which the human race is adjusted, at a given time and place. In the active areas of Earth, these temperatures are near what have been termed the "temperature optimum for human vitality."

As a part of his research on the influence of weather trends and cycles upon human affairs, Dr. Raymond Wheeler was once asked to comment on the matter of birthrates. His main points were as follows:

• The conception rate varies with temperature. Sterility in both sexes can be produced by excessive temperatures. The reproductive cells, especially those of the male, have less vitality at such times and develop defects.

• The birthrate also fluctuates with climatic change. Spontaneous high birthrates, both in humans and in animals, occur under certain definite climatic conditions and under no other conditions. The highest birthrates occur when it is cool or cold and wet, but not too cold.

The best times for high birthrates are during climatic transitions from the warm to the cold periods and from the cold to the warm periods in the one-hundred-year cycle. These are times of highest vigor, energy and best health of the reproductive cells. They are also times of greatest interest in children and family life. During these times people have large families.

• The same high energy level that produces an increased birthrate produces optimism and aggressiveness in the business world. As a result of this drive and confidence, competition increases, production increases and prices rise. This is boom time.

• The lowest birthrates occur when it is excessively hot and dry and when it is warm and moist (humid) for long periods of time.

• Those conceived in May or June lead more stable lives and accomplish more than those who were conceived in July – they also live, on the average, four months longer.

Those conceived in summer, in hot desert areas, die, on the average, ten years sooner than those conceived in the same area in early spring.

The eminent American scientist and historian, John W. Draper, said over one hundred years ago: "Where there are many climates, there will be many forms of men....For every climate and, indeed, for every geographic locality, there is an answering type of humanity."

Different climates of the world produce different kinds of plants and animals. The size, the color, the intelligence, the emotional stability, the tolerances, the philosophies, and the moral caliber of peoples are all basically determined by the climate or the prolonged weather trends to which they are subjected.

"Physicians, historians, philosophers, geographers, and statesmen in almost every century of history, since the time of ancient Greece, have recorded their opinion that man is profoundly affected by the climatic characteristics of his environment," Raymond Wheeler once wrote. "The interesting part is that these numerous observers have been in almost complete agreement regarding the main effects of climate on human nature.

"For example, they have agreed that people living in cool, temperate climates (not the frigid cold of Arctic or near-Arctic regions) are more vigorous, more aggressive and progressive, alert and persistent, stronger physically, larger, braver in battle, healthier and are less prone to sexual indulgence, although they have more children.

"In warm climates mankind was found to be more timid, smaller, physically weaker and less courageous, but more inclined to physical pleasures, including sexual indulgence, that they were more effeminate, lazier and less aggressive as well as less progressive. Scientists of the ancient and medieval worlds over a period of almost two thousand years expressed much the same opinion.

"No one doubts the correctness of this picture, in general, of the differences between cool (not too cold) climate and warm climate races and nations," Wheeler contends. "It is easier to reason with cool-climate peoples; they are more stable in their behavior and much more democratic, other things being equal. Every historian knows that slavery has never flourished in cool climates, but only in warm climates (unless in cool climates during excessive, but only temporary, warm periods). It is common knowledge that the brutalities inflicted upon underprivileged minorities; the blood-thirsty mutilations and tortures carried out among the members of royal families in the struggle for personal power; the bitter jealousies; the settling of differences by duels rather than by arbitration and compromise; the stabbings and other forms of murder, often on slight provocations; and cruel sex crimes of sundry kinds are all far more typical of warm countries than cool countries, but will reach a climax in cool countries during warm periods.

"We have noted that there is a strong tendency for state-promoted persecutions, pogroms and massacres to occur during the warm-dry phases of the one-hundred-year cycle. A graphic example is the horrible treatment by German officials of Jews and political offenders in Poland and Germany preceding and during World War II."

Warm climates or warm weather trends affect the sex life of people in two ways, according to Wheeler:

First, heat renders organisms more sensitive and delicate. Warm-climate peoples are less stable and more emotionally intense.

Second, they are more passionate, yet, on the whole, less fertile. They are more sex-conscious. On the other hand, sex is taken more for granted in cool-climate peoples.

There are different kinds of people living in different climates, with different habits, different mental and physical characteristics and different temperaments and philosophies of life. There are marked differences between people living in the warmer and the cooler countries. Indeed, the level of intelligence, fertility and the energy level of the population depend upon, and fluctuate directly with, the changes in the weather trends.

Whenever the climate of two cultures is similar, regardless of how distant they may be from one another, they enact scenes of analogous historical developments, even to economic attitudes and political behavior in general.

It has been said that if the history of humanity were to begin over again with the same biological factors and with the surfaces of Earth unchanged, history would be repeated in its larger outlines. The same trade routes, geographically determined, would determine the social and economic contacts of one race with another. These contacts would, in turn, create the same social and racial types. From this point of view, geography determines the character and evolution of human societies.

Effective progress depends upon the energy of the people involved. Climate reacts upon the people to stimulate energy.

The question becomes whether or not we can overcome the effects and vagaries of the weather. Can a population decide to act unimpeded by changes in climate?

7

The Stock Market and the Cell Barometer

In the book which he wrote with Og Mandino (*Cycles: The Mysterious Forces That Trigger Events*), Edward R. Dewey states that a "basic secret of nature" is that man is surrounded by cyclic forces that "bounce us like marionettes on a string." Dewey admits this concept is unsettling.

"Since it is demeaning to his self-esteem," Dewey writes, "it is perfectly understandable that man should resist any hypothesis that holds that his life and his universe vibrate in rhythms that are regular and at least partially predictable and are caused by a force or forces still unknown and possibly uncontrollable . . . .

"Nevertheless, the evidence that man is not one step down from the angels, sublimely in command of himself and his world, continues to accumulate. He is more like a character in a Punch and Judy show, pulled this way and that by environmental forces. And he will continue to be so manipulated until he solves the mystery of these forces. Only then will he be able to cut the strings and become himself."

John Cejka of Cyclomatic Engineering reminded me that the Maxwell-Wheeler research constituted a roadmap of time. "Our charts deal with the fixed distances in space between all points in a state. The time it takes you to get from one point to another depends upon how fast you can travel, right? You need to know the speed or the rate of motion and the time – these are your variables. The distance is fixed.

"Our weather maps are actually time maps. Time is a fixed quantity. The variables are space and motion. Understanding this, we can predict the future effects of weather just as you can predict the time it takes you to drive from Detroit to Chicago."

The Wheeler Culture Curve and the Maxwell Weather-Energy Cycle enable us to snip ourselves free from puppet status. When we possess a Roadmap of Time, we may not be able to alter curves in the highway, but we can prepare ourselves by knowing several miles away when the sharp bends will appear.

Perhaps nature cannot be controlled, but perhaps we can adapt to nature's whims and cyclic forces. The American Indian learned this basic truth of material plane existence generations ago, and the Native American has never been able to understand the European's arrogance toward the Earth Mother.

Cyclic forces are inevitable, but by knowing about them in advance through the Wheeler-Maxwell discoveries, we may exercise our freedom of choice and hold the cyclic result subject to our will. Knowledge of what is ahead for us on the recurring pattern of Time can enable us to prepare for adversity.

In an admittedly simplistic example, a group of men and women are suddenly transported from an area of perpetual warmth and sunshine to a land of seasonal change. Since they arrive in the summer months, they soon make their adjustments and begin to settle in what is to them a familiar pattern of existence.

But they do not know about winter. Their casual shelters offer no protection against freezing winds and snow. Their clothing is inadequate. Their meager food stores are soon exhausted. Quite likely, many of them would starve and freeze to death.

If we choose to structure our lives according to a linear unraveling of time, we will be as unprepared for the onslaught of crisis situations as were the unfortunate immigrants of the above example. If we can recognize the cyclic forces and their rhythmic intervals, we will be in the position of those who know that winter is coming.

There is nothing we can do about the cycle that creates winter, but we can prepare for the icy months by making warm clothing, winterizing our homes and putting up great stores of foodstuffs.

John Cejka quoted Raymond Wheeler about the question of free will: "[Man] fought the idea that the earth was not the center of the universe, not so much for religious reasons . . . but because he resisted the idea that his abode, especially to himself, was not the center around which the universe revolved. Steadfastly, in spite of a vast literature to the contrary, man has refused to place himself on the same plane as plants and animals in the great science of nature. . . . He will not take kindly to the fact that his behavior is extraordinarily sensitive to climatic influences. It will seem too much like surrendering intelligence and will to inexorable and mechanical laws.

"But this, again, will be a sheer rationalization. Man's dependence upon the laws of gravitation, of electricity, of the gas laws, of the laws of health and disease, has been the source of his emancipation – not the source of a fatalistic environmental determinism. Man's dependence upon climate and climatic change will become an added source of freedom if and when he will submit himself to the facts and turn those facts to his advantage. So long as he remains ignorant of these facts, he will continue to be a victim of the forces to which they point; but the instant he accepts the facts and proceeds to do something about them, his status as a victim will be transformed to the status of an intelligent agent – cooperating with the forces of his environment, rather than allowing them to govern him."

Maxwell found that there are high death periods tied to the weather. He found that the majority of men die when weather conditions are different from those prevailing when the majority of women die.

Elderly women pass away when there are intense variations or changes in air pressure. Men tend to die when there has existed a long period of low pressure.

Maxwell placed the reason for this on the "cell barometer." He held that every part of the human body is made up of cells which are self-contained tiny universes. Their outer skin may change shape, but, normally, remain the same size. He theorized that since low pressure must force something out of the cell for it to retain its size, it must have an expulsion of gases.

Cells are made up of liquids, gases, and other matter. Low barometric pressure causes an expansion, and since the body does not swell up during low-pressure periods, something has to be expelled from the cell. That something is gas, and part of that gas is oxygen. The cell, and therefore the human body, expells oxygen and other gases during low-pressure weather conditions.

So shoveling snow can compound a negative health condition. If one should have a heart attack while shoveling snow he or she would be rushed to the hospital and given oxygen. But because the body is busy expelling oxygen during this low-pressure period, it simply cannot accept the forced oxygen. The body is going to have to work even harder under stress conditions to expel the oxygen being pumped into the lungs. The only safe way to establish the oxygen balance would be to administer oxygen in an air-locked room, so as to isolate the treatment room from outside air pressure. Maxwell always maintained that operating rooms, recovery rooms and intensive-care units should be air-locked.

"I've verified the cell-barometer theory in my work with freeze-dried seeds and in other agricultural experiments," said John Cejka.

It could be that the cell-barometer theory may be one of the most vital of all Maxwell's legacies. Through Maxwell's discovery, each man and woman can chart his or her own personal cycle with astonishing precision. Months in advance, you can map out which will be your good days and your bad days. You can know when to plan a trip, when to enter surgery, when to have a baby.

Cejka explained a bit further about each of us being able to chart our own personal cycle.

"It can be as elaborate as you want," he replied. "Just try a simple chart at first.

"Take a few minutes each evening to review the day just past. Was it a good day or a bad day in terms of your general mood, attitude, emotions? Were you depressed, happy, excited, sad, worried, grouchy, irritable?

"Draw a chart on graph paper and place a dot on the appropriate spot each day. Pretty soon you will have a regular, dot-connected chart which will indicate your ups and downs.

"After a month or so, you should begin to see a pattern emerging which will represent your natural mood-attitude-emotion rhythm.

"A few months more, as additional personal data accumulates, you should be able to peek into your own future and forecast your highs and lows.

"As you acquire greater knowledge concerning your personal cycle – and therefore yourself – you will see that even tough 'downer' days will pass. You can see where you can change certain things – such as not scheduling a party, a dental appointment, or an important meeting, when you will be in a low period – and prepare to face things which cannot be changed, such as that social engagement or business appointment scheduled by someone else."

If we can actually have accurate foreknowledge of future happenings on the time cycle – possibly even the swings of the stock market, what is to prevent everyone from using the principles outlined here and doing the same thing? Surely such foreknowledge would seriously disrupt the very cycles which one is attempting to exploit, and the market would certainly collapse.

John Cejka believes that anyone possessing this specialized data could predict the curves of the stock market. "But even though anyone acquiring this information has the *potential* to become wealthy, the person's own psychological and cell-barometer curves, among other things, will determine whether or not he or she will be able to use the information correctly.

"Many of our clients have asked (this) question. 'If all this information gets out and everyone starts following the cycle, will the cycles still be there?'

"Because *all* human events enter into these cycles, all that would happen is that the maximum altitude of the cycle would be deemphasized. We wouldn't lose a cycle at all, we would merely smooth it out. You cannot defy the law by which you made the prediction.

"Let us take the commodities market as a specific example. Remember one fundamental: The cycles are made by people who have participated in the market. It is a law of the marketplace that ninety percent or better of the traders lose money. You are not going to defy the law of time itself. You are using the past to predict the future. If you make one hundred forecasts for one hundred individuals, I will guarantee that ninety percent or better will still lose money.

"The marketplace is always two people – the buyer and the seller. The professional trader in Chicago always takes the opposite side of what the public wants to do. The public is always wrong. When the public becomes convinced that the market is ninety percent bullish, is going to go up, the next day it will collapse. That is mass mind in function.

"When I first began market trading, I heard that the market becomes so erratic that it becomes an absolute dilemma. But I saw that was because every trader pits himself against the market. He is in there not necessarily to make money. It is King of the Mountain stuff. Your intelligence above everyone else's. You can get eaten up in there just as if you were in a jungle.

"This may be figurative speculation on my part, but the point I want to make is that other factors – including very definite psychological factors – enter into these cycles. Human nature has not changed in all these thousands of years. That is why I count on these cycles.

"If mass mind were to will away such things as droughts and famines, they would probably cease to exist. But until mass consciousness has been elevated to that degree, such things as droughts will continue to occur. What we can do now is to utilize the weather-energy cycle to predict such occurrences.

"If you study these cycles and if you really believe that they truly predict the climate conditions of the future, then you will know that, for example, a drought really will occur in such-and-such a year. Once you know that a drought will occur, you can always take steps to protect yourself. As Abraham Lincoln once said, 'If you know where you have been and if you know where you are, you surely should know where you are going'. Maxwell and Wheeler found out where we are going by correlating all human affairs with the weather."

Edward R. Dewey writes: "The study of cycles *can never give complete foreknowledge.* There will always be accidental variations and noncyclic factors that will enter into every situation, no matter how much we know about cycles."

Dewey points out in regard to the stock market that nearly every transaction involves one correct and one incorrect forecast of the future price of that item. Nearly every commodity price or stock price is going to go either up or down in the next hour, or next day, or next week.

"Whenever a trade is made, one of the two parties involved, either the buyer or the seller, has guessed wrong...despite all the facts and advice...available," Dewey observes. "We will improve our results as we learn more about our mystery and its cause."

But the stock market is merely a readily apparent example. We can theoretically interpret the fluctuations in the stock market and all other cyclical events. However, as with all things, the interpretation is affected by the variable of potential human error.

8

Golden Ages of the Past

R aymond Wheeler and his research associates found that throughout history the weather has had so much bearing on people's lives that it has strongly influenced their attitudes, thoughts, moods, temperament, activities and behavior. The weather directly controls all human activities, causing men and women to experience cycles in direct conformity to the weather cycles.

Wheeler did not interpret the cycles as indicative of *complete* environmental determinism, but people evidently obtain energy (physical and mental) and motivation of an imperialistic, totalitarian and absolutistic character on one hand, and of a nonimperialistic, individualistic, and democratic character on the other – in part at least through the way in which we are integrated with our natural environment. The one pattern flows over to the other, inevitably, as climate shifts back and forth between warm and cold periods.

But a summation of the overall climatic effect is needed.

Types of Behavior During the Transition from Cold to Warm

A period of high human energy level. Wheeler's intensive study makes it appear obvious that something about opposite extremes of temperature produces opposite extremes in collective human behavior. The association of these extremes of temperature with dryness or lack of action in the environment has something to do with human decadence.

The shift from a long cold period to a warm one – or, better, the sequence of these two conditions – has something to do with an increase or release of human energy that produces "better" modes of behavior.

"With increased vigor as a base (whatever the physiological causes may be), optimum conditions for an abundance of available energy for work occur during the period of climatic normality and on the upward crossing, or transition, from cold to warm," Dr. Wheeler declared. "This is the 'springtime' of the climatic cycle, while the preceding cold period was the 'wintertime'. On the upswing, more than in any other place on the cycle, the human race possesses energy, above that necessary for a maintenance of the physiological engine."

Maximum of human vitality as revealed in aggressiveness, longevity, high birthrate and low incidence of illness. "Here, mental and physical energy alike are at a maximum: hence the appearance of both good leadership and good followership; economic and political aggressiveness and enthusiasm; ability to exercise more self-control and make better judgments; predominance of constructive measures; and the absence of decadent modes of behavior. With all of these are associated a greater incidence of genius, a generally higher birthrate, a more stable behavior, and a higher moral tone of society."

A temporary lengthening of the sunspot cycle and a reduction in the number and size of spots for the duration of the warm phase, the beginning of a rainfall maximum with a long period of good crops; a period of maximum storms and floods. "Moreover, physical conditions are then the most favorable for economic prosperity and for the growth of stationary societies, dominated by city life, for rainfall is ample and crops are good."

A great majority of the best leaders in history: better than 90 percent of the sovereigns who have been given the title "the Great." The overwhelming majority of leaders who ruled during these times have received critical acclaim as great rulers by historians. Eighty percent of the rulers positioned at this place on the curve have been judged good by historians. These are the leaders of the revivals of civilization, the birth or rebirth of empires, nations and governments.

Nearly all of the names are located on the upward slant of the curve, between the midline and the rising side of the peak. This is nation-building time, a time of prosperity, a time of the best governments, that come at the midline on the upward swings of the curve and last through the first part of the warm periods, while it is still raining.

End of a civil war period and the beginning of an international war period associated with rising national spirit, charged with patriotism; nation-building and fresh processes of union; imperialistic conquests. It was Dr. Raymond Wheeler's theory that, without exception, governments or states revive from periods of disintegration and civil war on climatic upswings – from the cold-dry to the warm-wet phases of the climatic cycle.

It is during these periods, Dr. Wheeler maintains, that man rediscovers the advantages of union, cooperation and the division of labor. But cooperation is impossible without an increase in governmental control and centralization. Based upon available excess energy – with its resulting optimism, enthusiasm and aggressiveness – political unities form; imperialism and national feeling rise up; and international wars break out.

During nation-building times, the great international wars are fought with conquest as their aim. They are conducted with the aid of spontaneous enthusiasm and patriotism of the people and the armies.

Among the great nation-building wars of history have been the conquests of Cyrus the Great, in the middle 500s B.C.; the building of the great empire in India by Asoka the Great around 280 B.C.; the First, Second and Third Punic Wars between Rome and Carthage, each of which was fought on three successive peaks between 300 and 150 B.C.; the conquests first of Pompey and then of Julius Caesar; the conquests of Charlemagne, A.D. 780–800; the rule of Alfred the Great in the late 800s; the conquest of England by William the Conqueror, 1066; the conquests of Casimir the Great of Poland in the early 1300s, and at the same time the conquests of the Incas in South America; the wars between Louis XIV and Europe in the late 1600s; the Napoleonic Wars and the War of 1812; and, finally, World War I.

These illustrate the great outbursts of energy on the main climatic swings from cold to warm, which occur on the average of every one hundred years. Climatic, physiological, psychological, economic and political causes, all integrated in a single pattern, then "conspire" to produce strong and vigorous cultures, states and kingdoms.

Climax of the brilliant, Golden Age period, and less dramatic and far-reaching cultural revivals that follow the Golden Age patterns; revival of learning and a great outcropping of geniuses in the arts and sciences. When the upward transition is from a long cold period to a long warm one, a people, nation or empire, somewhere – frequently several at one time – enters upon what historians have called a Golden Age of cultural enlightenment and achievement, of which strong, but constructive, government is a part. During these brilliant cultural periods, national spirit in its best spontaneous expression arises.

In almost every century, just as the world climate swings from cold to warm, a Golden Age appears. This usually happens about the turn of the century, so that the first quarter is usually what Wheeler calls "the springtime of the century."

Simultaneously, there comes a shift from mechanistic to wholistic culture. In general areas, the following trends are seen:

Philosophy: rationalism, deduction, idealism, teleology, purposivism, mysticism, "wholism," wholistic laws.

Science: organic conceptions of nature, wholistic biology, epigenesis; "The plant makes its cells, the cells do not make the plant"; ecology; relativity; search for universal laws; the unity of the entire universe; universal equations; "field theory"; emphasis on pattern and system, coordination, integration. Geometry as opposed to algebra: areas, spaces, masses, as opposed to individual numbers and infinitesimals.

Social science: world views, universal histories, emphasis on cooperation as opposed to competition, emphasis on the state rather than on the individual; socialism, communism.

Psychology: wholistic theories, personality as a whole, social adjustment, the subconscious, learning by insight and understanding rather than by repetition; introspection.

The following are some of the more important historical periods that have occurred in this phase of the one-hundred-year cycle:

1. The age of the pyramid builders in Egypt, around 2500 B.C.

2. The age of the temple builders in Egypt, around 1500 B.C.

3. Cycle 3, one of the most famous of all time, extended from around 505 to 420 B.C. and encompassed the centers of two successive cold periods in the one-hundred-year cycle. (In those days the cold periods were short, and the warm periods long. Soon, however, the situation changed, and the warm and cold periods became more nearly the same length.)

During the rise in temperature from cold period to warm period in Cycle 3, there occurred one of the most profound of all the Golden Ages in history.

The Greek city-states blossomed into prosperous communities under the leadership of Athens. One of the basic features of this awakening and upsurge of vitality was a great industrial revolution. With this revolution came a period of unprecedented prosperity. Athens acquired control of the commerce of the Mediterranean and sold her wares, including pottery and products of iron and silver, over a wide area. The Greek colonies became wealthy also, and their size and number were greatly expanded.

Cycle 3 brought with it a worldwide awakening and a worldwide prosperity, comparable on the cycle to the prosperity of the early twentieth century, before the crash of 1929.

The worldwide awakening around 500 B.C. included many nations and empires. Persia tried to subdue the Greeks and succeeded in taking some of their colonies at the eastern end of the Mediterranean.

China enjoyed a period of awakening, strong government and prosperity in what was then primitive Japan.

There were strong nations south of the Black Sea, in what is now northern Turkey.

The indigenous civilizations, in both North and South America, were prosperous and were enjoying a cultural revival. Egypt staged an important revival. A strong state called Thrace emerged in the area now occupied by Bulgaria and Romania.

The brilliant phase of all this activity was over by 430 B.C. These were "New Deal" times, times of subsidies. It was apparently getting warmer all the time. A Greek architect and town planner, Hippodamus, advocated utopian socialistic schemes. Despotism increased rapidly everywhere, as did atrocities and massacres, just as they increased in Germany and Russia in our own times as it became warmer – and also drier. The birthrate declined as it did in the modern world during the late 1920s and in the 1930s.

4. The Ptolemaic age of Egypt, 200 B.C. Three historically important events must be noted during the boom days of Cycle 4, around 270 B.C. and the years that immediately followed.

One was the emergence of the brilliant Ptolemaic civilization in Egypt, during which Alexandria became a famous center of learning.

The second was the rise of the famous Asoka Empire in India, which became a period of unprecedented prosperity for large areas in that country.

The third was the rise of Rome to power, for it was during the prosperous phase of this cycle that Rome, with the First Punic War against Carthage, began her foreign conquests.

The records of history point to an era of prosperity in Palestine around 120 to 100 B.C., comparable to the era of prosperity we enjoyed in the late 1940s and early 1950s.

5. Rome at the time of Julius and Augustus Caesar, 60-15 B.C.

6. Building of the Eastern Roman Empire (Greek Byzantine) by Justinian around A.D. 527.

7. Founding of Charlemagne's empire, A.D. 771–814.

8. England in the days of Alfred the Great, 871–99.

9. England in the days of William the Conqueror, 1066.

10. The great empire of Genghis Khan, around 1220.

11. The Renaissance and great empire of the Spanish under Charles V, 1500.

12. England in the days of Elizabeth, 1580–1600 (the time of Shakespeare).

13. France under Napoleon and the United States under Washington, Adams and Jefferson.

The Industrial Revolution of 1800 occurred in exactly the same place on its own cycle.

Great wealth was acquired in all of the civilized world in the late nineteenth and early twentieth centuries when there was an industrial revolution, based on oil, steel and the assembly line.

14. The first quarter of the twentieth century: the building of the modern world.

Why all nations or people do not pass equally through a Golden Age on every climatic upswing is an enigma, but Dr. Wheeler felt that his laboriously achieved graphs indicate that all peoples improve to some extent at this time, while showing more aggressiveness in a political and military fashion. Civilizations too primitive to have a scientific or written literature undoubtedly improve artistically, but it is certain that they improve their economic status – that is, their trade and commerce.

During these times, a population shift from the country into the cities usually takes place. Tariffs are then adopted to protect industrial development. There is rapid commercial development; industrial revolutions; a long period of prosperity and rising prices (probably two out of every three years having the properties of a boom); and building of great financial empires.

Golden Ages – history's best leadership, best governments and most prosperous times – occur on climatic upswings from the cold to the warm phases of a long climatic cycle, because this type of climatic change furnishes us with a maximum of intellectual and physical vitality. This vitality expresses itself in optimism, enthusiasm, aggressiveness, economic expansion, industrial and social revolution, unification, imperialism and international wars. The new government, once set up, is at first firm, but constructive, often tolerant.

Unfortunately, of course, when this sort of upswing comes, a tyrannical regime can bring about an age of "iron" rather than one of "gold." Some form of autocracy – absolutism, totalitarianism or centralization – begins to emerge on the climatic upswing and is in its best phase during the earlier (wet) part of the warm period.

Strong governments continue with a trend toward more and more centralization of power, paving the way for statism; beginning steps are made in the direction of deprivation of various freedoms.

The pattern of warm governments has transposed from one warm period to the next, but the details are different each time. Naturally the character of the political cycle has changed radically in content over the centuries, even though it has kept its form. Today the largest proportion in history of the population of the world shares in some way or another in the change of government.

"It is absurd to attempt an interpretation of history on the basis, alone, either of continuity or of discontinuity, for history is both, as in a propagated wave, where a deviation to one side of the axis is still an advance forward, even as the phase is changing," Dr. Wheeler said. "It is the form of the deviation back and forth that has changed but little, if any . . . . but the forward advance of the wave has meant vast changes in the content of the political and military process, as well as in the number of people participating in it directly."

Wheeler did not intend his picture of political cycles to be taken dogmatically, but to represent trends and to point out that the rise and fall, both of centralized and decentralized governments, is synchronized with the course of the climatic cycle. Even the more primitive warrior nations of the tropics have conformed to the same climatic transitions from the cold to the warm periods. The warm and cold periods of history are worldwide and carry the cycles of rising and falling governments with them.

And so it is that during warm times the individual is subordinated to the state, the part to the whole; whereas during cold times the state is subordinated to the individual, the whole to the part. This situation characterizes the entire cultural pattern.

9

Periods of Decline and Decay

A time-honored axiom is that after a good sovereign has ruled – or after a good government has run its course – the succeeding government is not as effective. The trend is almost always toward decay.

Moreover, the trend is often from constructive and benevolent rule toward tyranny, cruelty and decline – toward a less democratic regime.

Severe droughts and excessively high temperatures bring on great economic depressions; failure or collapse of existing economic systems. Also evident is a period of decline, decadence and decay in the moral tone of society: instability of the family pattern; low birthrate; increase of promiscuity and sexual perversions; increase in the divorce rate; growing belief that the state owes the individual a living; shift from interest in freedom to interest in security; less interest in doing a good day's work; less interest in craftsmanship; more pay for less work; communism; socialism; statism; absolutism in government; tyrants; dictatorship; pogroms; massacres; persecutions; totalitarianism; New Deals; public works; substitution of the state for the church.

And so it turned out that strong governments were typical of warm times. The strongest governments, however, are not always the best.

The strongest governments of history are often tyrannical, totalitarian and either fascistic or communistic. These governments seem to reach their climax during periods of highest temperatures and low rainfall – that is, during the hot-dry periods of history. "Good" governments decline and disappear as it gets warmer and drier. The decline reaches a climax during the hot droughts.

Since Aristotle's time, it has been observed that governments tend to pass through cycles. A democratic government will work well for a time, then it will fall into the hands of a tyrannical bureaucracy from which it declines into a tyrannical plutocracy, or oligarchy, headed by dictatorship. A civil war brings back democracy, and the cycle is repeated.

"It was only on the upswing and during the early part of the warm period that strong governments manifested 'good' qualities such as liberality, constructiveness, benevolence, humanitarianism, foresight and stability," Wheeler wrote. As the period becomes hotter and drier, this type of government becomes decadent and tyrannical, along with a general cultural breakdown.

Wheeler often said that his purpose was not to evaluate, but to relate the facts as he interpreted them from his studies. He wished "merely to point out the similarity of the pattern throughout history that has prevailed during warm times as it pertains to the relation of the governors to the governed." Since the picture is essentially the same during every warm period, and is always the opposite during very cold periods, climate must have something to do with the condition of the political structure.

It is during the warm-dry phase that serious economic breakdowns, epidemics of dictators and leftist movements come into being. Fascism, totalitarianism, regimentation and absolutism have reached their climaxes during these periods in history. The government becomes more and more strict, an inevitable final phase of the unification process.

But this would not happen, or at least would not progress very far, unless the general weather pattern continued warm. As it becomes warmer, the centralization of power accelerates. Overexpansion and imperialism exhaust the nation just as it becomes warm, dry and physically debilitating. Economic depression and hot drought, coming consistently together, produce pessimism, lethargy, a willingness – even a demand – for government aid, which means socialism or communism.

The climate leads to social and mental instability, which will lead either to extreme lethargy, complacency, lack of loyalty on the one hand, or to fanaticism and an artificial, explosive patriotism on the other. It may even lead to both, depending upon the circumstances. The whole culture pattern becomes sordid and decadent; the birthrate collapses; stature declines. The people lack the energy with which to resist mob emotionality, with which properly to evaluate individual life, even with which to make good judgments. Hence organized intolerance and hatred reach a climax.

Communism, socialism and despotism, with or without a loyal majority of the populace, appear during periods of high temperatures. The result, of necessity, is either the dole or forced labor under a dictator.

This growth is pushed along under its own gathering momentum, until, as Dr. Wheeler expresses it, the haves separate from the have-nots. Opposed factions or parties emerge – each gathering strength in the general growth process. The haves, the aristocrats and conservatives, become fewer and fewer, but gain more and more in power at the expense of the many.

"As the warm period continues, as imperialism increases, and as the state becomes militarized, the reactionary movement becomes absolutistic and totalitarian, whether under a king, a duce, a fuhrer or a 'dictatorship of the proletariat.' The latter, by the way, is a complete misnomer as far as realities are concerned. There is no such thing as a dictatorship of the proletariat. The only way in which the proletariat has ever 'ruled' at any time in history – and the only way in which it can rule – is through truly democratic instruments."

During such phases, people willingly ask for such political movements. They lack the drive and the will to participate responsibly in a complex society. They blissfully hand more and more responsibility to their government. Religion becomes corroded in much the same manner. The church goes into decline, and religion becomes little more than a code of social ethics.

Likewise, societies become ill because the individuals within them are not in as good mental or physical condition as they are in other phases of the cycle. Because they lack vitality and stability, men and women do things which, at other times, they would strongly repudiate.

But after a period of lethargy and hardship, it turns cold. With this change (including the preceding drier years) come hardship and economic recession.

At first there is discontent; but, since it has been too warm, this discontent is more or less inarticulate and unaggressive. Besides, by now the government has its machinery set up to compel obedience.

After it has become cold enough – at or just below the longtime regional mean – the general energy level picks up. The haves and have-nots, constituting a conservative and liberal party from the upper strata of society to the lower, come into conflict. There is civil war. The old order of government is either removed or modified. A new order of government, with reform measures and a new leadership, comes to power.

"Thus, when it turns cold, the individual thinks of himself first," Dr. Wheeler observed. "A combination of increased energy, hardship, discontent; an overcentralized and tyrannical government; disgust with growing decadence, spurs him to fight for his individual rights. Here comes the realization that society can be improved only through the work and free expression of the capable individual. . . ."

This period is not a true cold epoch, Dr. Wheeler was careful to explain. It is only a break in a warm period. Revitalized physically and to some extent freed politically (in the long run the more democratic of the conflicting parties always wins when it is cold, especially on climatic downswings to cold periods), societies take a new lease on life. It turns warm; a reborn national spirit goes on another rampage, and a new outburst of imperialism precipitates more international wars.

Meanwhile, the new party has taken over the machinery of the old government. There has not been time for adequate democratic reforms. The existence of a strong opposing party makes it necessary to maintain a strict government. The growth that began on the first upswing continues. Now, perhaps, the state has a dictator instead of a king. At any rate, it exhausts itself in another series of wars and upsets its internal economy, just before the human energy level is bound to drop. Extreme temperatures and droughts lie just ahead.

One of Dr. Wheeler's points is that nations, like people, may become physically and mentally ill, grow weak and break down:

"There are, in general, two categories into which forms of insanity fall. While these are not inclusive, they cover the majority of cases. The one category includes depression, lethargy, seclusion, flight from reality, indifference, lack of emotional tone, schizophrenia, inaction. The other includes elation, overactivity, mania, excessive emotionality, belligerance and dangerous forms of paranoia. Mental deterioration or decline, then, expresses itself either way, dividing most individuals into these two psychotic groups. On the other hand, the normal individual will fluctuate, under pressure, from one mood – the depressed and indifferent – to the other – the manic and overactive. In an extreme form, either mood is a sign of weakness.

"Societies revealed many of the same characteristics when they became unstable, or went into decline, on the warm side; for it was here that there broke out fanaticism, cruelty, and intolerance as measured by inquisitions, persecutions, pogroms, massacres, and tortures, all state-promoted. Either indifference or fanaticism in a people, then, is a sign of weakness.

"It turned out that the more democratic countries or states generally declined through indifference, while the totalitarian and more dynamic states declined through fanaticism. The first political 'psychosis' was more often Western and the latter, Eastern; or, the first characterized the older states that had gone through several cycles: the second, the younger states of more recent unification. In any case, the appearance of these traits was certain indication of an imminent collapse into civil war."

The warm-dry periods in history have included the following:

1. Circa 540 B.C. The Age of Tyrants in the days of ancient Greece.

2. During the cold period centering on 420 B.C., the friends of democracy attempted to stem the tide of rising despotism; but the cold period did not last long enough. It turned warm again. Warm times breed regimentation and totalitarianism. At 404 B.C., for a year, there occurred the so-called Rule of the Thirty Tyrants.

Along with the growth of absolutism on the warm side of the climatic cycle, various associated phenomena invariably occurred – some form of socialism or communism. State socialism developed hand-in-hand with Spartan militarism and imperialism, until the family pattern practically disappeared. As the so-called Athenian Empire grew and as the dominance by Athens increased, her institutions became more and more socialistic. State socialism in the ancient world assumed the form of state militarism.

3. 330–320 B.C., a period very similar to the 1930s. Philip of Macedon and his son, Alexander, were the Hitlers of that time. The states and empires of the world were all in a condition of decline and were despotic and reactionary. In 323 B.C. thousands were banished from Athens by the Macedonians; and in 320 B.C. Jerusalem was taken by the Egyptians and thousands were deported.

When the warm phase of this cycle had run its course toward the end of the 300s B.C., a long cold period set in and governments began to collapse. Alexander's empire broke up. Civil wars raged everywhere.

4. 200–190 B.C. In Egypt there was severe oppression. The Macedonians pillaged Greece, burning schools and defacing monuments. The Aetolian League of city-states pillaged Sparta.

5. A.D. 85–95. Domitian, a cruel despot of the Roman Empire, came to power and persecuted the Christians. Hardly had the Roman Republic become a monarchy than the armies determined who should be the emperor. The man who could control the army controlled the state. Then the state was obliged to care for the discharged legions and their families.

6. A.D. 585–600. Mayan civilization in Central America was in a state of decadence; religion was reactionary and stereotyped; the priesthood was fascistic and "rancid." Spain turned Athanasian and burned all literature of the Arian Christians, Justinian's government persecuted all Arian Christians, Jews, and pagans. There was a cruel and despotic ruler in China. Tyranny and cruelty was rife in the Frankish kingdom.

7. 800–810. Charlemagne's government became reactionary. This was a period of laxity and decline in the Arabian kingdom of Baghdad. In China serious economic depression was caused by overissue of bank notes.

8. 1000–1030. This time was primarily warm and dry. Ghazni princes invaded Hindustan, creating great carnage and desecration of the temples. The Danes were in England. Basil, King of the Greek Empire, put out the eyes of fifteen thousand Bulgarians. Jews were banished from England. China was a virtually socialistic-militaristic state. Hakim of Egypt destroyed the Christian churches of Syria.

9. 1255–1270. The kingdom of Castile went bankrupt. Popular government was abolished in Florence.

There was a depression in the 1250s to 1260s during a time when it was mostly warm and dry. This period was similar to the 1930s.

The situation in England at the time was described as "a period of great economic distress." Town finances in France were in a chaotic condition.

This was a fascistic and communistic period in history, as in the 1930s. Crops were poor; there were numerous famines; and there were persecutions of the Jews. Governments were despotic, costly and dissipated.

10. 1365–1375. In England workers could work only at a certain price under penalty of the pillory or the loss of an ear. Noncompliance meant being branded with a "V" for "vagabond." If the worker attempted to escape, he or she was branded with an "S" and made a slave for life. If the worker then protested, he or she was hanged.

The sequence of events in Europe and other parts of the world in the second half of the 1200s and in the early 1300s is comparable to the sequence of events that the modern world is passing through.

11. 1630s. In England, Parliament was forbidden to discuss or question any state edict. It was then dissolved for eleven years. Degenerate phase of the Thirty Years' war. Great cruelty exhibited by the Turkish ruler. The Poles persecuted the Greek Orthodox Christians. Tolerance decreased for all forms of Christianity in England except the official church. Roger Williams went to Rhode Island to seek freedom.

12. 1670s and 1680s. Fascism and tyranny were the rule in France under Louis XIV and in India under Alamgir I. South Carolina adopted Indian slavery. Massachusetts was deprived of its charter.

An economic recovery accompanied the return of rainfall around 1690. War then broke out between France and England. The American phase of this conflict is known as King William's War.

At the end of this wet period, namely, in the first decade of the 1700s, the price of wheat fell, and again it was warm and dry. It was at this time, in Cycle 25, that a situation comparable to World War II developed. A war broke out between Louis XIV of France and several of the other European countries because Louis wanted to add Spain to his domain.

13. 1930s. Dictators present all over the world. Their creeds took different names – Russia: communism; Germany: Nazism; Italy: fascism. Many countries changed their form of government from democracy to a dictatorship. A devastating worldwide economic depression raged. During World War II prisoners of war were treated as slaves. Persecution of Jews in Germany. Extreme temperatures and droughts worldwide.

Government reached its most deplorable condition during the hot drought period that terminated a warm epoch. The shift toward tyranny was plainly evident even in warm periods of only ten years' duration. Rulers who were benevolent on the upswing always became fascistic if their rule extended into a warm-dry period of any length.

On the other hand, notice that there are names such as Alexander the Great just before 300 B.C.; Diocletian just before A.D. 300; and Stalin, 1930; who belong to the latter parts of the peaks. Still, these were times of dictatorships. Such times were followed by civil war and the collapse of governments, as temperatures shifted to the cold side.

We are beginning the twenty-seventh distinct recurrence of this trend in human affairs since the days of ancient Greece.

"Again a combination of causes – economic, political, psychological, biological, and climatic – leads to the next phase in the cycle of events," Wheeler stated. "Before political unity has declined, and while fanatacism is still controlling governmental policy, temperatures start dropping; and the national spirit revives and plays into the hands of a decadent and despotic leadership. Thus imperialism bursts forth once more, and international wars break out on the warm side of the downswing."

According to Wheeler's analysis, wars that come at the end of the drought period have always been the worst wars of history from the standpoint of a disregard for human life. Here is where the majority of the "senseless" wars have been fought; where kings or generals have led their men to the slaughter for a cause that would have been scorned on the upswing; where populations have been disregarded; where noncombatants, women, and children have always been looked upon with the least respect; where the greatest massacres have occurred; where marauding and looting have been at their worst.

More humane attitudes have always been shown on upswing wars. An "international law" of some sort has usually played a part, even though the fighting at that time is usually the hardest.

During downswing wars, there have always been more betrayals, more fifth-column activity, more lethargy on the part of the invaded, more welcoming of the invader and more dictatorial manipulation of discontented populations.

"All of this results from the fact that, whenever and wherever it is warm for an extended period, the individual becomes less important," Dr. Wheeler commented. "It is then that he is killed with the least compulsion; it is then that fanatic sacrifice for the state reaches its highest pitch under the right combination of circumstances."

10

Times of Civil Strife

Thus it would appear in the vast research materials assembled by Dr. Wheeler that absolutism, socialism, communism and totalitarianism, on the one hand, and democracy, individualism and laissez-faire government, on the other – the two opposite types of social organization – are definitely conditioned by opposite types of climate.

A democracy will not last through or develop during a warm period.

Absolutism, tyranny, socialism, and communism will not last or develop through a cold period.

In the normal course of history, as temperatures continue to drop, it becomes more stormy and more invigorating. The mounting discontent with government, plus a possible economic exhaustion or defeat in an international war, or both, combined with the continued drop in temperature, lead to the next phase of events.

Since this phase occurs at no other time than with a drop in temperature, the stimulating, but also irritating, influence of a changing climate is an essential factor in the picture. A temporarily increasing rainfall, and decreasing temperature, bring personal discomfort, because the winters are long and cold, with many storms.

While still warm, but under lowered temperatures and increased rainfall, we find an outbreak of international wars, usually promoted by the dictator nations (less democratic and more fanatic). These are often called "nation-falling wars" because governments are in the course of collapsing; these wars are more cruel than the nation-building wars; prisoners and populations are either slaughtered or enslaved; race antagonism reaches new highs; there is disregard for efforts to control war; and promises and treaties become worthless. It became evident to Dr. Wheeler that governments gradually decayed, in one manner or another, as the warm periods continued; but that little or nothing was ever done to prevent this development until it turned cold.

Also characteristic of cold-wet times are:

• Appearance of large sunspots and a temporary shortening of the sunspot cycle, presaging the shift from the warm phase to the cold. Appearances of the aurora, of which there would have been only a few visible at temperate latitudes during the previous warm phase; lowering temperatures and increasing rainfall; beginning of a second period of storms and floods.

• Sudden and marked increase in the birthrate; period of high energy level; great improvement in health in population at large; general increase in alertness, initiative and aggressiveness of the individual in all areas of human action and achievement; betterment in the moral tone of society.

• Migrations from the cities to the country; a return to the land; shifting of homes and industry to the country and to undeveloped areas. Beginning of migration from one country to another; cultural intermingling and borrowing.

• Revival of foreign trade and investments; increase in travel for both business and pleasure; period of inflation; high prices; prosperity; economic booms. Business boom periods also come at the end of a warm cycle when temperatures are falling and the cold-wet cycle is beginning. Another extended period of prosperity and high prices begins, but in general the price trend is downward. As the cold period advances, human energy again decreases and another depression occurs before it starts turning warm. (We were in such a period in 1975.)

• Decline and decadence of the old aristocracy and ruling class; reactionism whether the government is an absolute monarchy, a republic, or a socialistic dictatorship; decentralizing trends in government, business, the church and in other basic human institutions; antitrust movements. Great religious leaders who advocate the dignity and importance of the individual are typical of cold times. Jesus lived during cold times, as did Confucius and Mohammed. A period of emancipation, democratic reforms and revolutions; new and more liberal constitutions; inauguration of constitutional government; civil rights legislation; removal of restrictions; overthrow of despotic governments and dictators; climax of management-labor problems; strikes and other labor difficulties; liberalization of laws and religious creeds; reform movements in religion; return of laissez-faire thinking and policies; revival of private enterprise; reaction against socialistic and fascistic trends; anti-satanism.

• Termination of international wars and beginning of a long period of rebellions, revolts, insurrections, coups d'etat, palace revolutions and murders, party struggles, factionalism, sectionalism, religious controversies and wars, race riots; vigilantes, assassins, Ku Klux Klans and secret societies are on the upswing. There are sometimes great wars fought on the falling side of the curve, at nation-crumbling time, but these lack the enthusiasm of nation-building wars and are often successful only with the aid of fifth columns. The stage is set for rebellions and civil wars. The old national spirit, the old loyalties, are rapidly disappearing. There is disillusionment. It is decided that the hopes entertained in the previous outburst of nationalism were false; the masses are bitter. Anarchy increases.

"Consistently," Wheeler wrote, "during the better phase of democratic movements, tolerance, Christianity, interest in education, cooperativeness, enthusiasm for the individual, and orderliness prevailed. There was much travel, cultural borrowing, and an extension of trade. The breakdown took the form of anarchy, intolerance both of outsiders and of one another, race and class riots, assassinations, and sabotage. During cold times the government usually attempted to control the persecutions of racial or other minorities; but during the warm droughts, these have practically always been government-sanctioned or government-promoted events.

"Just as the antecedents of political communism were serfdom and slavery, so the antecedents of democracy were piracy and anarchy. Societies during the cold periods of ancient times were in a state of complete disruption. There was little or no central government. Populations were at a minimum. Many cities were empty, deserted, or in ruins. Marauding bands and migrating hordes ravaged the countryside and pillaged the towns. The seas were infested with pirates.

"The next step was taken when depopulated civilizations were able to survive under some degree of order during cold times by maintaining trade routes and colonies and mercenary soldiers as protectors of commerce. Towns were protected by garrisons to ward off robber barons and guerrilla bands. Knights in castles, surrounded by their serfs, protected themselves and their vassals as best they could against one another and wandering tribes. Commerce was hindered by thousands of local tariff barriers and tolls; profits were reduced by the necessity of paying tributes for being left unmolested. Each community had its own laws, coins, weights, and measures. Life was insecure at best. Rival cities or small principalities fought one another over their commerce until it became apparent to the wiser among them that prosperity could not exist without order or justice.

"When state governments were in the early stages of their development and standing armies had been organized, these armies frequently broke loose during cold times and became pillagers and marauders, headed even by members of the nobility. Secret societies of assassins, ex-soldiers, and adventurers carried on an unhindered piracy on land, while sea pirates patrolled the seas. Political parties fought wars of annihilation; among the nobility, feuds were common that hurled loyal followers into senseless bloodshed.

"In short, there has been a pattern on the cold side that has transposed from one cold period to another down through history, a pattern whose extreme form has been anarchy pure and simple, ranging from wars, intrigue, and treachery among the governors and their loyal followers to commercial war, race and religious riots, and armed civil war among the governed. All this is the fanatic aspect of cold times. The 'lethargic' aspect has always assumed the form of neglect, debauchery, and extravagance on the part of the rulers and the upper classes, and listlessness, pauperism, begging, itineracy, license, rapine, and vagabondage among the lower classes."

Normally, after a succession of serious droughts in the center of the cold period, the rains begin. The rains, together with cool temperatures (the midline represents temperatures in the temperate zones of around 50°F), raise the vitality of the people of all classes to its highest level, just as the curve reaches the midline on its upward swing. The most severe rainfall occurs at the midline.

Civil wars, fought after the tyranny has become intolerable, coincide with the drop of temperature into a cold period. These civil wars result in democracy – or at least in democratic reforms. In the extreme case the condition in some instances is anarchy, out of which democracy in its best state emerges. This may come during the earlier part of a cold period, but generally toward the end.

Sometimes the governments are able to sustain themselves, but eventually they will fall – if it stays cold. In spite of democratic reforms, leadership is generally lacking and frequently corrupt. Meanwhile, as one might expect during a period in which the individual life is rediscovered, society becomes flippant and none too orderly.

This is the true Romantic phase of history, with its appropriate literature, art and costume emphasizing the individual's rights, feelings and self-expression. Thus, there is a reaction against the old order, against the old aristocracy and everything it produced. Culture becomes superficial, but out of it a new order emerges, a new commerce, a new leadership of better quality.

Sovereigns during cold civil war times are not likely to rule very long. They are often assassinated or run out of office after being in power a short time. Governments change hands rapidly during cold times. Even during the long reign of Queen Victoria during the cold mid-nineteenth century, party government changed hands numerous times.

There are, of course, leaders noted for their constructive work during civil war times. These leaders promote democratic forms of government, or they are patriots who lead the struggle for civil rights. Such were the Gracchi in Rome, shortly after 200 B.C.; Marius, shortly after 100 B.C.; Hus, the fighter for religious freedom in Bohemia right after A.D. 1400; Cromwell in England in the middle 1600s; and Abraham Lincoln in the United States in the middle 1800s. But there are not nearly as many of these earnest reformers as there are good leaders of nation-building time on the upward slant of the curve.

A strong, far-seeing, and democratically-minded ruler has at times been able to pilot a state through the downswing, through the civil war epoch, and been able to give the citizenry needed democratic reforms. Certain Norwegian and Danish rulers seemed to have been able to do this. Peter the Great combined the qualities of a tyrant and reformer, and probably kept Russia free from anarchy. Lincoln gave promise of being a good downswing leader; Andrew Jackson was not.

The following are famous cold-wet periods in history:

1. 320–310 B.C. Alexander the Great, at nation-falling time in the late 300s B.C., carved out a shaky empire that, with his death, collapsed into civil war. The famous Chandragupta expelled the Greeks from India and paved the way for a recovery of India.

2. 140–130 B.C. Jerusalem under Simon the High Priest. In Rome, the revolutions of the Gracchi took place in interest of democratic reform.

3. A.D. 0–30, which contained many cold-wet years resulted in worldwide revolts. The teachings of Christ, with emphasis on worthiness of the individual life, started to be spread.

4. Conquests by Attila the Hun in the first half of the fifth century A.D. contributed to the fall of Rome.

There are regularly two main periods of prosperity in each of the one-hundred-year cycles. One comes on the upswing of temperature from the cold to the warm phase. The other occurs on the downswing of temperature from warm to cold, where we were in the late 1940s. However, the documents of the past covering the second part of the cycle are not as complete as those covering the first part. This is primarily because governments were crumbling and about to collapse. Revolutions, insurrections and civil wars were brewing.

On the other hand, during the swing from cold to warm, governments are strong and better records are kept. By the Middle Ages, however, more detailed information and indisputable evidence have been left to indicate that periods of prosperity, such as the one we have just left, have been regular occurrences down through history.

A thousand years ago on the cycle we find a comparable time sequence. It was at the beginning of a long cold phase in Cycle 17, and the first weavers and fullers (cloth thickeners) were established in the Belgian city of Ghent. The textile industry expanded rapidly in western Europe. Private enterprise was encouraged in England and by rulers elsewhere. Merchants began a long struggle for freedom and power against the nobility, which they eventually won. Feudalism became the economic and political pattern of the later Middle Ages.

Those were extremely dynamic times, and the civilized world was seething with change. The Norsemen of Scandinavia and the Slavs of Bohemia were beginning to embrace Christianity. The Norse and Slav cultures were merging in Russia, as were those of the Saxons and Danes in England. A new world was being born and an old world was dying.

The new system, feudalism, was to last five hundred years.

In Japan the provincial military class of society sprang up.

Chinese classics were printed for the first time by means of wooden blocks as a cheap substitute for stone engraving.

What was to become the oldest continuous parliamentary body in existence was established in Iceland.

There was a great awakening in Germany under Otto the Great, which marked the beginning of the Holy Roman Empire.

Exploration and migration dominated the scene. Civil wars were fought everywhere. There were violent disputes between the monks and the clergy, between emperors and popes, between the new and old classes of the nobility, between invading hordes and the native populations. China hurled back hordes of Tartars bearing down from the northwest. Norse and Russians sailed down the Dnieper River to the Black Sea. The Arabs invaded India.

5. 1035–1045. Ferdinand the Great united Leon and Castile after subduing the rebellious barons. Holy Roman Empire was at the height of its power; it was an era of great prosperity in the towns. The Truce of God was declared by the Pope to minimize private wars. In Norway, Magnus the Good, an outstanding ruler, came to power.

6. 1100–1105. In England, Henry I granted the Charter of Liberties, removing abuses of previous tyrannical governments. Milan declared itself a republic.

7. 1134–1140. In Aragon, representatives of the cities were summoned to the assemblies, an important step in the evolution of democratic government. Power in the Holy Roman Empire was transferred from the Emperor to the Diet. Louis VII supported a communal movement in France, a movement based in local self-government.

8. 1130–1175. This was a period containing many cold-wet years. In Denmark, the reign of Waldemar the Great brought about many prosperous years. The Bank of Venice was created. In England, the great Council and the Constitution of Clarendon brought secular control to the

clerical courts. This time also saw the beginning of trial by jury, beginning of the grand- and petit-jury systems, recognition of the common law and circuit judges. Venice became a great maritime power.

9. 1215. Strife between the barons and King John of England led to the signing of the Magna Charta.

10. 1280–1290. As a result of the depressions, tyranny, and finally, the falling temperatures, a great period of democratic reform took place.

In the 1280s and 1290s, an era approximately concurrent with the cycle we are now in, the Magna Charta was reaffirmed after having been repudiated. Model parliaments were instituted in England and France. Numerous legal reforms were achieved. In 1283 an equivalent to the Magna Charta was exacted from the King of Aragon in Spain. The famous Italian poet Dante was instrumental in effecting democratic reforms in Florence.

These particular hard times came during a period, generally, of great democratic reforms. They are comparable to the depressions in the modern world during the mid-nineteenth century, which was also a time of great democratic reform. They are also comparable to the depressions that occurred in the late 1950s, the late 1960s, and which lie ahead in the 1980s.

11. 1420–1430. The Hussite wars were fought for religious freedom. In Poland, the right of habeas corpus – in which citizens cannot be imprisoned without trial – was established.

12. 1640s. In England, the famous war between Parliament and the Crown (Cromwell) took place.

13. 1680s. The "socialistic" state system of economy and mercantilism had run its course under the despotic rule of Louis XIV and other totalitarians. In Turkey the Shah handed over the government to his wife, who did as she pleased while he lived a life of voluptuous pleasure. Louis XV came to the throne of France, but he was indifferent to the welfare of the country. In Poland the government reached such a low ebb that little work was done and no laws passed in two generations because of the unscrupulous youth of the country who predominated in the Diet and ruled with absolute power.

Centering on 1710, there was a strong boom in the same place on the cycle where we were in 1952. Temperatures had fallen, shifting back and forth across the midline between the warm and the cold side as temperatures did in the late 1940s and early 1950s. A brief cold-wet phase developed. Speculation went wild. There was a strong revival of private enterprise.

So it went around the world; but nevertheless, it was a time of temporary prosperity, while governments changed hands. The price of British wheat more than doubled during this boom and wet period. Numerous new business adventures and speculations were undertaken; and, for a while, they prospered.

14. 1810s. Revolutions in Latin America leading to independence.

15. 1830s. Revolts and rebellions worldwide. In France there was revolution in Paris. In the United States there was the Jacksonian movement. California and Texas revolted against Mexico. Greece and Holland became independent. Slavery was abolished in British colonies. Reform bills were introduced in England.

16. The 1860s. The American Civil War was fought. Other civil wars were fought in Poland, Italy, Japan, and elsewhere.

17. The 1880s. Various constitutional reforms and liberalized governments were instituted around the world.

18. The late 1940s. There was economic prosperity in many countries of the world; rapid economic recovery in war-devastated countries; inflation. There were widespread labor strikes and civil strife in Palestine, India, Greece, Burma, Java and China. There were troubles in Italy, France, and many Latin American countries. Increasing resistance to Russian tyranny developed in the Balkans. There were signs of increasing internal dissatisfaction in Russia. Dissatisfaction in England was growing toward leftist regime. Resistance was growing in the United States toward leftist trends.

All of these events and occurrences reached a speed and intensity that happens only once in five hundred years – in the 400s, the 900s, the 1400s, and now, the 1900s.

History is repeating itself at a higher level of technological, economic, and political progress than ever before; but, nevertheless, it is repeating itself.

The conquests of Tamerlane in the late 1300s; the last wars of Louis XIV in the early 1700s; and World War II in which Hitler, like Alexander the Great, attempted to carve out an empire, come at nation-crumbling time. We are still in such a period.

The cycle can lead us to predict that all governments that did not change after World War II will do so not far in the future.

The three major events of the political cycle – (1) the strong, constructive government of the upswing; (2) the despotic and decadent government of warm-dry times; (3) the decentralized, often "anarchistic," but democratic government of cold times – are products of the relative amounts of human energy that can be processed for achievement, and of the sequence of high and low energy levels. These levels are determined in the main by climatic conditions.

According to Dr. Wheeler, "Three major facts pertain to the rise and fall of governments, that, all through the investigation, were so invariable and their relationship to climate so precise as to challenge an attempt at an explanation in general terms.

"First, there were the occurrence of Golden Ages, the rise of strong governments under superior leaders, the outburst of imperialism and international wars on climatic upswings from long cold periods into the warm-wet phase of the climatic cycle.

"Second, the decline, onset of decadence, the growing excesses of centralized government, the emergence of dictators, tyranny, fanaticism, communism, and socialism, as the warm epoch continued, and as temperature and dryness increased.

"Third, the occurrence of civil wars, rebellions, and revolutions, the origin and growth of democratic institutions and individualism, during cold periods. . . . No law of chance can explain the fact that undemocratic trends are invariably associated with the warmer climatic phases, and democratic trends with the colder phases. No law of chance can explain why international wars so consistently predominate on the warm side and civil wars on the cold. Relationships so consistent, universal, and precise point directly to a causal factor or set of causal factors."

11

Challenges of the Cold-Dry Years

Some form of increased democracy – individualism, liberty or laissez-faire government – emerges on the climatic downswing, and is at first anarchistic in the sense of civil war and its aftermath. Then for a time democracy is at its best, especially if good leadership is available. This is generally during the later part of the cold period near the upswing, provided the upswing is not too dry and warm. But the more democratic type of government is inclined to decay during the cold-dry period.

The data on weather-energy cycles continually indicated to Dr. Wheeler that after a dull period during the cold droughts, when democracy became decadent and the "me first" spirit led to an intolerable state of corrupt and wasteful affairs, the climate begins its climb to the next warm epoch.

Democratic institutions emerge from a cold period because the individual's discontent is backed by a sufficient amount of aggressiveness, individual spontaneity, interest and optimism. Despots are no longer tolerated, because the invigorated individual thinks of his or her rights first, and of social welfare second. When the individual is lazy and incompetent, he or she thinks of the state first, because all the person wants is to be fed and to be taken care of by the state.

If, at such a time, conditions promote a secondary revival of national spirit, the willing subordination of the individual to the state plays directly into the hands of fanaticism. At that point, the political structure goes to absolutistic or communistic extremes. From the standpoint of individual freedom, the one type of government is the same as the other. Both are totalitarian in political control and authority.

Dark Ages and periods of superficial culture have always occurred during cold periods. But there was a gain as well that transcended the loss. After each cold period, civilization reached higher levels of achievement than during the previous warm period.

"The Golden Ages of history, the best in human health and leadership, cultural output, the great periods of economic and political growth and expansion, have occurred after a toughening process has been going on that has revitalized the race at the biological level," Dr. Wheeler writes. "Moreover, during cold times cultures came in contact with one another during migrations, travel exploration and colonization—all of which extended to some extent into the earlier part of the warm period."

"In the hands of a new generation, a fresh national spirit wells up, and revolts occur against frustration," Dr. Wheeler asserted. "Enthusiasm, optimism, and aggressiveness, organized through a social revolution, result in a new state. . . . As democratic government continues, it tends to become bureaucratic—either in the hands of leftovers from the previously dominant aristocracy . . . or in the hands of a new generation of rulers who have come into power through intrigue, wealth or some other form of leverage. A new set of rebellions break out following the dry years of the cold side; and during these rebellions, effort is made to overcome the evils of decadence in the democratic pattern, or the tyranny left over from previous warm times. . . .

"A strong leader comes to the front. A new Golden Age is on, and a new cycle of imperialism begins. The revolutions result at first in democratic reforms, because they begin on the cold side. Were it to remain cold, these reforms would remain; but as it becomes warmer, the more power the 'radical' party assumes.

"After a reign of terror, the new spirit coalesces into a strong, centralized government that, from the standpoint of individual rights, is reactionary."

Cold-dry conditions include:

• Long droughts during years of low average temperatures (conditions that did much to stir up the great migrations of the past).

• Continuation of the cold-wet trends.

• Climax of migrations and immigration. Climax of cultural intermingling and borrowing. Democratic trends go to an extreme; a climax of anarchy, piracy, vigilantes, democracy out of control; general weakness in government; climax of religious controversies.

• Increase in foreign trade continues; emphasis on free trade. Long period of economic depressions and low prices; business good in about one out of every three years.

• Era of immoral rulers and sovereigns. Tendency for another period of decadence to develop, this time within the mechanistic, democratic pattern as opposed to the wholistic, autocratic pattern.

• Shift from the stadium principle in recreation and in athletics to the Olympic principle, emphasizing more participation of the individual. Revival of religion; evangelism as opposed to social ethics and abstract religious philosophy; revival of emphasis on the individual conscience and the relationship of the individual to God; Sunday school movements; resurgence of hymn writing and religious music, music that is to be sung by the people as opposed to symphonic music.

• Feminism; labor movements; international workers' associations and like organizations. All through the cold period, a general awakening of the "proletariat," or masses of the people; rapid improvement in intelligence and knowledge; spread of educational institutions; increase in free public education; gradual re-emergence of national feeling; revival of folklore; wider use of local languages as opposed to the language of the aristocratic class; conquered countries and races acquire freedom.

• At the end of the cold period after the droughts are over and rainfall has picked up, and with temperatures rising, a fresh outbreak of revolutions set up new and strong governments which in one way or another are always more democratic than any previous governments; final overthrow of the old tyrannies; the new governments, benevolent and democratic as most of them are, initiate the process of restoring regimentation and tyranny as the cycle in government repeats itself; the period of nation building again, the period of Golden Ages and the Renaissance phase of the culture cycle; and there is the threat of international wars as temperatures approach their longtime averages and cross to the warm side.

Some of the famous cold-dry periods of history were:

1. 310–290 B.C. Furious civil war and anarchy in the empire of Alexander the Great. Migrations and piracy.

2. 185–155 B.C. Corrupt Sparta finally looked to Roman yoke with relief. Syrian bands overran Palestine; religious wars broke out among the Jews; Maccabeus finally expelled the Syrians.

3. A.D. 50–70. In Rome, Nero was in power. It was a period of short-lived emporers and Jewish revolts.

4. 170–200. Anarchy all over the world. Rome was in a state of disintegration. Numerous migrations over Europe and Asia.

5. 445–480. Downfall of the ancient world, including fall of Rome. Attila's great empire fell apart. Anarchy and religious wars were fought in China. England invaded by the Jutes. Huns, Gepidae, Goths, Langobards, and others roamed central Europe.

6. 630–690. This period was cold and dry, but with a considerable number of cold-wet years. Religious wars fought among the Arabs and victory of Mohammed. Period of "do nothing" kings in the Frankish kingdom. Anarchy worldwide.

7. 840–880. Violent civil wars everywhere. Charlemagne's empire crumbled and was divided. Beginning of the feudal system. The Norsemen overran Europe. Beginning of what is Russia.

8. 930–985. Great social and economic changes as feudalism was established. End of first half of the Middle Ages, terminating a five-hundred-year cycle. Anarchy, piracy and civil war were universal. Spread of Christianity and new forms of private enterprise. Ethelstan, King of Wessex, encouraged private enterprise. Corruption rife in the Church.

9. 1460–1490. Fall of the Middle Ages and a great climax to many civil wars. In England, the Wars of the Roses and the end of feudalism heralded the beginning of a more democratic system. In Japan, the peasant class almost disappeared as a result of the long civil wars. Civilizations in the Western Hemisphere were in a state of disruption. The status of the Holy Roman Emperor was reduced to nothing.

10. 1715–1745. In the late 1710s it turned cold and dry, just as it began to do in the first half of the 1960s. A French investment and real estate promotion known as the Mississippi Scheme – an early example of modern speculative finance – suddenly collapsed, bringing widespread panic and disaster. At the same time a British speculation scheme that came to be known as the "South Sea Bubble" burst, causing a panic in England.

The period of prosperity and speculation was as wide as civilization – as was the resultant economic decline. In some places it was much worse than in others. Trade declined between Spain and Latin America. In 1720 the British wheat price hit another low. Civil wars were fought in Persia, Turkey, Hungary, China, Russia, Ceylon, Mongolia, Morocco, Bulgaria, Tibet, North Africa and the Philippines. Tensions began to develop that later were to crop out in the American and French revolutions.

11. 1780s. This was a period of various difficulties in the American colonies following the revolution. There was an indifference toward the new union. Tension was rapidly mounting in France. There was worldwide civil strife.

12. Late 1880s and 1890s. Anarchist movements were widespread in Europe and the United States. Numerous revolts in progress, but they were especially violent in Cuba, Philippines, Russia, Chile, Argentina, Egypt, South Africa, Brazil and Panama. Labor movements were popular. The "Gay Nineties" illustrate the glitter and garishness of cold-dry periods.

In locating these different cultural events in relation to the climate curve, "exceptions" will be found. That is, an event that typically occurs during a warm period may appear a little ahead of time or may continue into the beginning of the cold period.

Where exceptions occur, we must understand why they occur. Since the climate curve is a generalized one representing the world as a whole, and since the different areas of the Earth do not shift from the warm to the cold or cold to the warm side at exactly the same time, not every item will fit unerringly into the phase of the climatic cycle in which it might be expected.

A discrepancy of this sort might mean that the climatic phase was a few years ahead or behind what occurred in most of the world; therefore causing societal changes in some parts of the world while other sections displayed the characteristics of another climate.

A discrepancy might also mean that local conditions, over and above the weather trends, have sensitized scientists, artists, political leaders – or even the population of the area as a whole – in such a manner that they responded more quickly, even to slight changes in the weather trends, than did the populations in other countries. At almost any time there are individuals, especially in science or in art, who anticipate a major trend and act on it.

Social, economic, and political forces in their own right, or the personality of a particular leader, may even cut across the influence of the longtime weather trends and alter the usual timing of the event by the weather factors. Social and political institutions tend to perpetuate themselves by means of their own inertia.

A given event or the work of a given individual is often "transitional" in character: it is partly "warm" and partly "cold." In many instances, a given person or group outlives a particular warm or cold period and, although generally under difficulties, continues on within the pattern of the previous phase.

The one-hundred-year cycle may contract and expand at times (ninety to one hundred ten years), but it averages close to one hundred years and has maintained that central figure down through history. There is every reason to suspect that the cycle will continue to behave in this fashion.

Most importantly, there has not been an extended cold-dry period since the nineteenth century, but we have just now entered such a time, which will continue to the year 2000.

12

The Specter of World Famine and Financial Depression

In a two-part feature for *Science News,* John H. Douglas warned that broad-based food reserves and new technological advances are needed to stave off worldwide famine. Douglas reports grimly that global food reserves are at their lowest level in two decades and that "with malevolent coincidence" the world's climate has begun to change.

Douglas quotes weather scientists who say that the Earth's average temperature has lowered 2.7° F since 1945. Weather over the last half of this century has been the warmest in a thousand years and a cycle of colder temperatures can be expected to follow this warm trend. There will be a major shift of rain patterns and deserts. The northern latitudes will be faced with a shorter growing season — just when a starving world will be looking for more food from their fields.

According to a study conducted under the aegis of the United Nations, more than 700 million people in less-developed countries are suffering from malnutrition. All experts unequivocally state that the leadership of the United States will be essential in checking world famine and sustaining a reasonable standard of living for those millions.

In eight years, 1965 to 1972, the United States provided 84 percent of all food aid contributed by industrial nations, according to figures compiled by the U.S. Agriculture Department. Now, because of increasingly tight food supplies, both citizens and politicians are beginning to feel a bit less generous about the stock in our own dwindling larder. Resentment has also begun to grow against India, the single largest recipient of past food aid, as that nation fails to show concern for population control and recently directed vital funds away from food productivity into the development of its first nuclear weapon.

Indian Prime Minister Indira Gandhi has observed: "In any discussion of the future of mankind, we cannot afford to underemphasize that its vast majority lives in what is called the developing world. Despite the natural resources and traditional cultures of their lands, this huge segment of humanity is condemned to poverty. If these millions cannot be assured of their basic essentials, what meaning can discussion of the protection of the environment or of preserving the ecological balance or of saving wildlife have for them?

"Can we ever hope to achieve a world free of tension if the greater portion of humanity lives in want, while a small affluent minority monopolizes the benefits of modern technology?"

J. Merrill Anderson, Iowa Farm Bureau leader, told farmers assembled for a conference in Des Moines that it was time for the United States to establish sound practices in its national and international policies before the greatest food-producing section of the world was inadvertently destroyed.

"Some well-intentioned people are advocating either elimination or substantial reduction in animal agriculture," Anderson remarked. "If we were to follow these suggestions, we would not get any more to the starving. We would bankrupt grain farmers and then produce less.

"However, we cannot ignore world suffering. The United States has pledged temporary food aid. We can give more technological and other types of assistance if [underprivileged nations] decide they will do what they must do to help themselves."

Anderson, who in November 1974, attended the world food conference in Rome, observed that official policies must have been wrong in the past; for although the United States has done more than any other nation to assist other countries, he heard nothing but vicious criticism of the United States. Anderson suggested consideration of a national policy of tough-minded humanism or tough-minded compassion:

"We will help these desperate people only if steps are taken to make lasting progress. It appears highly probable that giving food without any requirements will only result in more suffering in the long run."

Dr. Garrett Hardin, professor of human ecology at the University of California in Santa Barbara, suggests that the United States adopt a "lifeboat ethic." It is not possible to share wealth, Dr. Hardin points out, only poverty.

"So long as nations multiply at different rates, survival requires that we adopt the ethics of the lifeboat," Dr. Hardin told the *Chicago Tribune*

Magazine. "A lifeboat can only hold so many people. There are more than two billion wretched people in the world – ten times as many as the population of the U.S. It is literally beyond our ability to save them all . . . . Both international granaries and lax immigration policies must be rejected if we are to save something for our grandchildren."

Dr. J. George Harrar, president emeritus of the Rockefeller Foundation and principal architect of the "green revolution" that developed hybrid grains exceptionally responsive to fertilizers, foresees massive world famine if the United States should suffer one or two major crop failures. "Climatologists anticipate that, based on the cyclic nature of the weather, North America could well have a severe drought in the near future. I'm scared. We could have a lot of starvation . . . . It is unrealistic to think this could not happen."

Some financial experts are predicting a market crash that will make 1929 seem mild by comparison. Even with some current improvement, inflation is forcing men and women to spend so much on the necessities that luxury and leisure items are being left on the market. Increasing scarcity of raw materials and inexpensive food will keep prices arching upward and continue to fuel inflation. There is a terrible economic crunch coming, these financial pessimists warn, and everyone is going to be affected.

We are facing difficult times in weather trends in the approaching cycles. There will be dramatic changes in world conditions – political, cultural, and economic – which are of great importance to every one of us. All of this is presaged by the following:

• World temperatures are falling.

• We are now in the cold phase of a one-hundred-year cycle. The remainder of this century will be spent on the cold side of the longtime average.

• Accompanying the drop in temperature will be long, severe droughts.

• After the cold phase has passed, world temperatures will probably begin to climb. The resumption of warmer weather will be accompanied by a great abundance of rainfall, after which there will perhaps be a recurrence of droughts such as those of the 1930s.

• At that time, there may occur the heat climax of a thousand-year cycle (the previous heat climax occurred around A.D. 1000). After the heat climax, which should peak in the 2040s, it may be that the northern lands will begin freezing up again.

The December 1982 issue of *Science Digest* presented a summation of the various scientific theories that predict that another ice age is coming soon. Although the last great ice sheet retreated about ten thousand years ago, experts say that we are living in a warm interglacial period. The Earth's climatic pendulum, according to Dr. John Gribbin, is set to swing us back to an ice age within the next five thousand years.

The Earth *is* getting colder. Why?

Perhaps because of a global wobble caused by the gravitational tug of the Sun and the Moon on the planet's equatorial bulge, which causes the Earth's axis to shift, to tilt, even to change its orbit from elliptical to nearly circular and back to elliptical.

Or maybe because of what is known as the "Greenhouse Effect."

"In the atmosphere," Dr. Gribbin explains, "carbon dioxide acts much like the glass in a greenhouse: it serves as a radiation trap, allowing the sun's rays to penetrate to the ground but blocking the escape of the reflected heat energy into space."

Various plant life, such as blue-green algae, thrive in such an environment and reproduce at remarkable rates. It has been said that a single algae cell, under ideal conditions, could generate a colony with a mass equal to that of Earth in two weeks. Such a proliferation of plant life, Dr. Gribbin points out, could almost totally deplete the carbon dioxide in the atmosphere:

"Heat would rapidly escape, chilling the Earth and initiating a glacial epoch. . . . By one estimate, merely cutting in half today's quantity of atmospheric CO_2 (0.03 percent) would trigger an ice age."

Another popular theory regarding our coming ice age concerns itself with "veils of dust" that may originate from our own planet (ash from volcanic eruptions) or from gigantic clouds of interstellar dust that blight our planet with each turn of the galaxy. In either event, temperatures on Earth would drop when the debris comes between Earth and the Sun.

Then, although it sounds like science fiction, there is the concept of a magnetic pole reversal. Actually, magnetic north has not always been north. As many as 171 times in the past 76 million years, the magnetic poles have reversed themselves, with north becoming south, south becoming north.

"It is widely thought that Earth's magnetic field is somehow related to climate," Dr. Gribbin comments. "Advocates of this theory have linked some of the magnetic reversals to major climatic changes that have triggered the birth or death of an ice age. . . . Scientists predict that we will undoubtedly undergo another reversal sometime in the future; whether this will actually generate an ice age remains to be seen."

In Wheeler's assessment of the recurring cycles, every other five-hundred-year period in history is dominated by Western civilization. Every intervening five-hundred-year period is dominated by Eastern civilization.

Dr. Wheeler found that at the end of every other five-hundred-year cycle, major revolutions occur over the entire world and result in drastic reorganizations of society. According to this projection, we are in a revolution of this sort now, comparable to the collapse of medieval culture and the beginning of the modern world.

The Maxwell-Wheeler research indicates that societies all over the world become seriously ill at least once every one hundred years, desperately so every five hundred years. Every five hundred years, the one-hundred-year sickness rhythm and the five-hundred-year sickness rhythm converge. That is happening right now.

One of the symptoms of such a convergence is an unusually severe depression. Another is the moral tone of society – especially its manner of rearing its children. There are hundreds of these symptoms: the kind of art prevailing at the time, the emergence of state socialism, decadence in the government.

Now in the 1980s, the five-hundred-year era that has belonged to Europe and her offspring, North America, is coming to an end. If the cycles repeat, the next five hundred years of history may belong to Asia.

"It seems highly certain," Dr. Raymond Wheeler wrote, "that the initiative is again passing from the West to the East for a five-hundred-year period, as it did one thousand years ago and two thousand years ago. All of Asia is waking from a sleep of five hundred years. Needless to say, the future of America is tied into this great convulsion and must be appraised in terms of it, or not at all."

The present five-hundred-year cycle ended in 1980. The changes that are now taking place will, of necessity, alter many of our patterns of behavior. Our economic system and the world of business are not exempt.

It was Dr. Wheeler's contention that one should always seek to obtain a general view of things so that the more specific and concrete happenings may be fully understood.

"The latter derive their meaning from the former," he observed. "The parts derive their meaning from the whole."

In order to better understand the events of today and tomorrow, Wheeler advised, one should study occurrences at the termination of previous five-hundred-year cycles.

"While specific events do not repeat themselves in history, types of events unquestionably do," he commented.

All of the signs point to a continued repetition of this rhythm – which means that the rest of this century is due to be severely cold. We are now into the cold phase of the one-hundred-year cycle and the fifth and severest cold phase of the five-hundred-year cycle.

Today, once again, as another five-hundred-year cycle is drawing to a close, outworn institutions and outmoded patterns of thought are no longer adequate. Once more we are heading into a cold period that marks the end of a cycle in our historical epoch.

In fact, *the twentieth century may be a crucial period in the history of civilization.*

In the coming centuries, climatic changes will become more severe, the warm and cold phases longer. This will mean more violent transitions from one side to the other, with an increase in storminess, floods and, doubtless, an increase in events such as earthquakes and volcanic eruptions. This will also mean longer warm-wet periods with an increased danger of tropical diseases, longer droughts with greatly lowered human vitality, and a greatly reduced birthrate.

In addition, unless political structures are stabilized, there is the possibility of rule by intolerable tyrants during late warm times, and a degeneration into piracy and anarchy during cold times. Such effects could produce undreamed-of slaughter and costs during unimaginably horrible world wars during the climatic transitions. This would also mean devastating economic depressions with unheard-of suffering and want.

But on an even larger scale, if his interpretation of the data is correct — and if the longtime process of acceleration has reached its limit or nearly so — Wheeler feels that the only conceivable expectancy is that of a reversal to a long series of decelerating cycles during which climate will deviate more and more from optimum conditions. Eventually, the decelerating process would reach the point at which the temperate zone would become tropical or semi-tropical on one side of the axis and severely cold, perhaps cold enough for ice ages, on the other side.

"It would seem more than a matter of wild speculation that this assumed reversal of climatic cycles may be upon the human race within the twentieth century," Wheeler declares.

In the February 1981 issue of *The Futurist,* John Platt, a general systems theorist who previously taught at the Universities of Chicago and Michigan and who is now a lecturer at the Boston University School of Medicine, stated his theory that physical evolution is in a process of acceleration. In his *The Acceleration of Evolution,* Platt writes that we may be history's most unique generation:

"This general conclusion that the present generation is unique within so vast an evolutionary frame may be resisted by believers in the constancy-theory of history or in the cyclical or cultural rise-and-fall theories. It is often asserted, for example, that the apparent speeding-up and increased scale of technical jumps today is just a phenomenon resulting from our selective emphasis on more recent events. But . . . such a view is no longer tenable. Jumps by so many orders of magnitude in so many areas, with this unprecedented coincidence of several such jumps at the same time, and these unique disturbances of the planet, surely indicate that we are not passing through a smooth cyclical or acceleration process similar to those in the historical past.

"Anyone who is willing to admit that there have been sudden jumps in evolution or human history, such as the invention of agriculture or the Industrial Revolution, must conclude from this evidence that we are passing through another such jump far more concentrated and more intense than these and of far greater evolutionary importance. . . .

From my reading of Raymond Wheeler's unpublished journals, I know that he would not find John Platt's allegation to be at all diametrically opposed to the cyclical theory of weather-energy and history that he and Maxwell espoused. In fact, Wheeler set forth such a notion of acceleration decades before Platt suggested it.

As he was grappling with what would appear to be mysterious "gaps" in the prehistoric flow of the cycles, Wheeler decided that the only reasonable solution could be that the cycles had, on occasion, stepped up, or reversed, themselves.

Wheeler went on to theorize that such a reversal of the time cycles had occurred three times in the past and that profound evolutionary events had occurred during each cyclic fluctuation.

During the first reversal, the various vertebrate species of animals evolved. The basic physiological structure of these creatures made them better able to deal with the climate and conditions of the emerging Mesozoic Era. Had the vertebrate pattern not stabilized in relation to environmental forces, Wheeler speculates, it might well have been extinguished altogether during this era.

During the second climatic optimum, Wheeler tells us, another profound step in evolution occurred – the emergence of the mammal and primate patterns and the beginning of prehuman forms.

Then writes Wheeler, "The primate pattern had developed sufficiently by the end of the last ice age to permit a third profound occurrence during that series of rapid and mild fluctuations. This profound occurrence was the emergence of modern man and his psychological and social achievements."

Purely as a heuristic principle, Wheeler points out, the deceleration-acceleration theory of the history of Earth's climate is worth further investigation.

"There are possible implications that have an important bearing upon human problems today," he suggests. "This would mean that a new and probably different series of similar general form will soon begin, and thus Earth is about to begin a new phase of its history."

Wheeler would have been in complete agreement with John Platt's speculation that . . .

"We may be passing through a 'birth canal' to some new kind of life. In the last ten years we have begun to see radical changes into new directions everywhere, yet we also realize that the moment of birth is the most dangerous moment of the baby's existence. In the first few seconds or minutes, it must learn to do things it has never done in the womb – to breathe, to cry, to swallow and so on. If it fails to do any of these things successfully, it dies. So today we must learn to manage several new global powers and problems with which we have had no previous experience – problems of world order, the environment, the biological balance – or we may kill ourselves."

If we are about to undergo the fourth cyclic reversal and if the first three reversals introduced new life forms, what dramatic evolutionary changes might we be about to witness?

Wheeler says that this cyclic reversal, falling as it may during the cold-dry period we are now entering, will be "difficult to live through." If the history of climate as outlined by Wheeler should repeat itself, he warns that the cycle will be accompanied by an increase in the severity of earthquakes and volcano activity that accompanied the dropping of continental attitudes. He also expects flooding on the upswings and mountain building on the downswings.

In other words, Raymond Wheeler's portrait of the last twenty years of our century is very much like that revealed in the "Earth Changes" material of the psychic Edgar Cayce, the Native American prophecies of a Time of Great Cleansing and the interpretation many fundamentalist Christians place on apocalyptic passages in the Book of Revelation.

Jay Ogilvy, professor of philosophy and author of *Many Dimensional Man: Decentralizing Self, Society and the Sacred,* told journalist Peggy Taylor that he perceived the '80s as a time of crisis, not apocalypse.

"Not everything coming to a halt, but, because of the energy crunch, some of the ruts that we first resisted, but then kind of settled into, may just come to an end. We'll have moved from a luxury of choices to a paucity of choices, and finally to a necessity for choices. We are really going to have to make some changes."

Behind the need for changes and choices, Ogilvy sees a shift of consciousness: "Our vision of the world is shifting away from seeing the world as a kind of great clockworks, with God as the cosmic Clockmaker – a vision in which we think if we can just find the right levers, the right pulleys, we can make things happen according to the light of reason. I think we're finding that we're not living in a great big clockworks, but in a swamp, sharing a kind of ecological interdependence, so that now, instead of saying, 'None of us is free until we're all free' (as we said so optimistically in the '60s), we're saying, 'If any of us makes a mess, we're all in a mess.'

" . . . In the '80s we might see something like a 'we generation': different groups pursuing interests that are neither universal and altruistic, nor individual and selfish. . . .

"We're already witnessing the phenomenon of interest groups that have evolved beyond the shallow dialectic of altruism or selfishness. As people get together around any single cause, they discover that no single cause really sustains life. . . ."

Just as vertebrate life patterns led to mammalian forms and they, in turn, led to our immediate ancestors, we may be witnessing a fundamental change in the nature of the human race. However, it is very likely that rather than being a specific set of physical changes that this will be a consciousness shift. If the wide variety of social and climatic conditions are correct, this shift should lead to an increa   awareness . . . the value of total cooperation.

13

The Politics and Economy of the Future

Based on his research, which stressed the comparing and the contrasting of past cycles of weather energy and their effect upon all human affairs, Dr. Raymond Wheeler offered guidelines for Cycle 27 (see chart page 41), which we have now entered:

- There will be a prolonged period of civil strife, class struggle and civil wars all over the world, as trends shift to democracy. There will be temporary despotisms.

- Racial and religious minorities will demand more privileges of the state.

- The problem of states' rights will become a burning issue. Decentralization of the federal government will be demanded.

- Disorder will increase in the form of uncontrolled fraud, graft, rackets and swindling.

- There will be a revival of secret orders and societies, some of them bent on taking the law into their own hands. Mob violence, race riots and the like will be more frequent.

- Strikes will increase as labor becomes more and more demanding.

- All official forms of racial and religious discrimination will disappear in the United States and the other democratic countries.

• Unless they make drastic democratic adjustments to a rapidly changing world, the present ruling classes and parties of the world will disappear.

Mahbub ul Haq of the World Bank has commented, "We recognize the reality that nations of the world are increasingly interdependent; that there are definite limits to the unilateral actions of the power nations; that the time for genuine equality between nations has finally arrived; that the rich nations need the poor nations for future markets and for new economic frontiers while the poor nations need the rich nations for their capital and technology; and that we can together build the premises of a mutual partnership, not a permanent struggle."

If it is going to turn cold, Wheeler tells us, the political changes that will occur all over the world will be in the direction of democracy, and away from socialism and communism. Those countries that have scrapped their democratic constitutions will have to revive or rewrite them. Those countries which, already democratic, have centralized their political control and have limited local autonomies, will go through a decentralization process.

Wheeler said that the undemocratic countries will endure bloody civil wars. Most likely, Spain will suffer civil strife as another attempt is made to accomplish democratic reforms in that nation. There will be a succession of revolutions in the Latin American countries as more democratic forms of government and more democratic forms of economic control are being created.

All communistic governments will fall. Terrorism, mob violence and anarchy will hold sway until reforms have been effected in those countries which have supported communistic regimes.

Hazel Henderson, author of *Creating Alternative Futures,* has stated her opinion that traditional methods of measuring productivity ignore social issues and therefore are inadequate for making wise choices concerning economic activities:

"It is clear that a massive evolutionary shift is underway based on a radically new set of environmental and resource conditions, and that these conditions are driving human societies into domestic transitions and a new configuration of global order. This New World Order is inevitable, even if the keepers of the old order, in their fear of change and loss of their own power, try to stem the tides of change by means of desperation, violence, and nuclear war."

Both the warm and the cold periods of history have made their permanent and substantial contributions to the evolution of the modern state. Warm periods have furnished the concepts of cooperation, coordination and integration. Cold periods have furnished the equally necessary concepts of individual initiative and freedom. Neither will permanently give way to the other. If there is any attempt to change, the result, of necessity, will be a compromise between the two in their extreme forms.

The long-term outlook is a middle-of-the-road position, but the end of existing despotisms and international wars is near at hand. However, the beginning of a period of civil wars and rebellions is imminent.

No one can tell precisely how long the expected cold period will last. Should temperatures fail to drop consistently during the next few years, the onset of rebellions may be delayed, and the international wars may continue. But remember, climate is not the only cause of human affairs, even if it assuredly determines the main trends over a period of time.

A long cold period would doubtless mean a more or less complete democratization of the world – a type of democratization that would not abandon those features of centralized government and those social responsibilities of the state that history has demonstrated to be workable and desirable. It ought to mean the last of dictators forever.

We also must recognize that every alternate five-hundred-year cycle has been characterized by the domination of Europe. The intervening five-hundred-year cycles have been dominated by Asia. A five-hundred-year cycle which belonged to Europe is now terminating.

A study of historical cycles shows that a world convulsion is occurring that should be second only to the emergence of rational thought in the sixth century B.C.; the fall of Rome and other ancient civilizations in the fifth century; and the Renaissance after the collapse of the Middle Ages in the fifteenth century.

The coming convulsion is comparable to the birth of Christianity in the first century and the birth of the modern nation as a feudal principality in the tenth.

The next five-hundred-year cycle will be dominated by Asia. The parts of the world that will develop politically and economically during the next five-hundred-year cycle will be Oriental countries.

The warmer countries and areas of the world, including the southern United States, will experience a dramatic awakening. We must learn to be more tolerant and understanding of other people in our own country and people in other nations.

The cold-dry phase of the one-hundred-year cycle which we are about to enter is one of a long, or at least recurring, depression.

The cold-dry phases have been the Dark Ages of history. Civilizations have disintegrated during these periods. Chaos, anarchy and piracy have prevailed. The world has seethed with migrations. Orderly government and commerce have suffered.

Can we be prepared to alter such a firmly established pattern?

Economist Hazel Henderson has a kind of basic optimism about the future. In an interview with journalist Peggy Taylor, she commented, "I think we could make the '80s a period of rolling readjustment. And the way that we can ensure that that happens is if everybody takes a little more responsibility for their own lifestyle, for their own life, sees the context of this inevitable transition that we're going to have to go through to develop new patterns, a whole new productive system, based on sustained yield and renewable resources.

"The energy-conserving lifestyle that's needed now is actually something that we might enjoy *more*. Not only could we get through it very easily, if more people became activated to take that kind of responsibility I think we'd find it rewarding to reuse all these rusty qualities in ourselves – the earlier virtues of thrift and hard work, putting our shoulders to the wheel, getting back to more basics. I think we could end up with a much more satisfying society."

Difficult times have occurred in each of the twenty-six preceding cold-dry phases of the one-hundred-year cycle. We are now about to enter the twenty-seventh cold-dry phase since 575 B.C., and there seems no evidence to support hope for a time of economic prosperity. Although we can expect numerous problems from the recurrent cycle, we can also gain some knowledge of how to prepare ourselves.

If the cycle remains true during the next twenty years, one-third to one-half of the years will be severely cold and dry. The entire period should average on the cold and dry side.

Already the growing season is shortening.

In 1974 an early September frost destroyed millions of dollars' worth of maturing corn in the Midwest.

On August 11, 1982, what the United Press International labeled "brisk" Canadian air put down a carpet of frost in the upper midwestern United States and set record low temperatures.

It was an abrupt change from the traditionally hot "dog days" of August to record lows set from Buffalo, New York, to Kansas City, Missouri. Duluth, Minnesota had the lowest reading at 37 degrees.

Once the cold phase has stabilized, frosts in June and in August may occur regularly in the corn belt. Early and late frosts may become a serious menace in southern California, Texas, Florida and other parts of the Deep South. Winters will become so severe as to cause trouble for cattle and sheep raisers on the western ranges. Blizzards will become much more common than they have been for fifty years or more. Severe and lengthy droughts and famines will be worldwide.

Logically, there are a number of things we can do to prepare. The United States, and the world as well, should be preparing for long shortages in its water supplies and for shorter, not longer, growing seasons.

We must prepare for colder weather and long droughts, which, in turn, will bring about scarcity of food for the prosperous nations, famine and starvation for the less economically stable. It would be wise, therefore, for agricultural researchers to concentrate on developing cold-resistant plants and faster-growing crops—especially faster-growing corn and wheat—if normal yields are to be maintained.

The northwest plains and mountain states will probably suffer the most, but the north-central and northeastern states will receive their share of bitter winters and shorter growing seasons. The most prosperous part of the United States, agriculturally, might become the southeast or Gulf states.

Frosts will penetrate deeper into the ground over the upper two-thirds of the country, especially in the northern third. It would be well to make certain that water pipes are deep enough underground. There will be much more below-zero weather in the northern half of the country than during the last quarter of a century or more, and there will be more freezing weather in the southern half.

Along with the fall in temperature will come a serious decline in rainfall. This has happened consistently on the one-hundred-year cycle, twenty-six times since the days of ancient Greece. Each one of these longtime drops in temperature and rainfall shows in the sequoia tree-ring curves. The longest of these curves goes back to 1350 B.C.

In the fifth century, near the time when Rome fell, world rainfall was so low that the California sequoias grew very slowly for many decades. The Caspian Sea in Asia sank forty-five feet below its present level.

There are long cycles in rainfall just as there are long cycles in temperature. As in the case of the shorter cycles in temperature and rainfall, the longer ones follow, or parallel, one another. In the long run, temperature and rainfall fluctuate together. World rainfall is declining now, along with world temperatures. At the end of the century both will recover together.

Until then, however, agriculture and industry must prepare for serious trouble in regard to the national water supply. We are using water faster than nature can replace it. The water table is sinking quickly, everywhere. It will sink a lot faster and a lot farther in the decades to come.

It would behoove the nation to store and to conserve every available gallon of water. We may be forced to draw on the Great Lakes and on the oceans for water. Irrigation projects of undreamed-of scope may become necessary.

Remember that not only the United States and Canada will suffer, but the other continents as well. It will be necessary to develop drought-resistant, as well as cold-resistant, plants and crops.

Temperatures may fall for ten years or more, then start climbing again, only to fall once or twice more before the next longtime climb begins, which is not expected to begin until around 2000.

Obviously droughts and frost will have their effect on our economy — but remember that it, too, is directly linked to the weather cycle.

The decline of an old world, such as we will experience in the next few decades, is inevitably characterized by a succession of rapidly occurring and troublesome economic depressions. Times may have changed from the earlier terminations of five-hundred-year cycles, but the laws of nature have not.

We cannot expect any real upswing in worldwide financial conditions until the end of this cold-dry period. As average rainfall increases somewhere around 1995, the next era of prosperity will begin.

Severe and lengthy financial depressions will be worldwide. We must condition ourselves for recurring economic hard times.

The coming cold-dry depressions will not all be times of loss. According to Raymond Wheeler, they will be periods of the revival and the re-establishment of the free competitive system of economy that has always been destroyed by nationalism, dictatorship and severe depressions of the preceding warm-dry periods. Primitive and backward countries will experience rapid advances, along with unrest, and will undergo accelerated industrialization.

But the most important thing to remember is that the weather cycles indicate the beginning of a worldwide renaissance during the next major warm-wet phase beginning in the year 2000.

14

The New Golden Age

E ven though we face the prospect of great societal change in the next twenty years, we must remember that civilization has undergone four great convulsions through recorded history. Each time the world has emerged better than it was before – more stable, richer and with greater concern for individual rights. The period before us, although severely troubled economically, will witness great democratic reforms throughout the world.

"All this confusion is the reverse side of social reconstruction," Raymond Wheeler wrote. "Renewed faith in democracy takes root during these times. Emancipation of the underprivileged and oppressed occurs. The forgotten man is recalled and comes into his own as a *free individual*, not as a ward of the state! More important yet is a revival of religion and the spiritual power of whole peoples and nations, along with a shift from classical and abstract forms of artistic expression and literature of the romantic and concrete, extolling the importance of freedom and the individual."

As we near the beginning of the sixth five-hundred-year cycle, can we visualize what the democratic aspect of the coming revolution will bring?

Raymond Wheeler foresaw the rise of the laboring class to political and economic power.

"Heretofore," Wheeler tells us, "the working classes have had little to do with government and nothing to do with the means of production. The modern industrialized world is a product of the middle class. The

American and French revolutions were revolutions of the middle class, not of the factory worker, peasant or farmer. The modern world, thus far, has been a middle-class businessman's world."

Wheeler cautions us from becoming alarmed at what is really "a sign of progress." The demands to be made by labor in our closing decades of the fifth five-hundred-year cycle are only an extension of the principles of democracy into areas in which they have not previously been applied.

George Leonard, author of such works as *The Transformation,* and *The Ultimate Athlete,* told *New Age* magazine that the '80s were going to bring about the end of "automatic material prosperity, the end of automatic material progress," which, in his opinion, would be one of the most serious psychological problems ever faced by a culture.

It will be exceedingly difficult, Leonard reflected, getting people used to the idea that they are no longer going to be rewarded with material progress.

"Assuming this kind of change happens," Leonard speculated, "and given the present tax structure, the people who are going to be seriously injured will be the people at the bottom end of the scale. . . .

"I'd like to see a single tax system which would take care of both welfare and social security and which would get rid of a lot of the loopholes – and would also promote a slow-growth instead of a fast-growth economy."

Leonard foresees that the future must see us focusing not on GNP (Gross National Product) but on GNS (Gross National Satisfaction).

"A transformation on the part of the people is also implied. It's all tied together – the antinuclear protests, people who are interested in the environment, those who are interested in peace. . . .

"Conservation is the answer, and conservation ultimately implies a transformation. Conservation means turning away from exponential growth. And once you turn away from exponential growth, you have a different psychology, a different way of being in the world. We *could* go toward a police state which allocates increasingly rare and short supplies – but I don't think we want to go that way. Or we can bring about a transformation in which we voluntarily turn our attention to the things we've put aside all these years while we've been playing with these trivial material toys."

Wheeler acknowledges the potential danger of a dictatorship following a revolution of the proletariat, because the laboring class lacks the means, knowledge and experience to construct a real democracy.

"Freed from the tyranny of a monarchical form of government, chaos would reign without some new form of despotism to take the place of the old," Wheeler warns.

The high standard of living in the United States has produced better-educated working classes than elsewhere in the world, Wheeler observes. Therefore, "it is inevitable under these circumstances that they should want to share in running the economy of this country. They are rapidly acquiring the knowledge and the capacity to take a direct part in this process."

Wheeler firmly points out to management that there is no turning back the hands of the great cosmic clock.

"The most constructive thing that management can do," he advises, "is to accept the inevitable. It must see to it that labor in this country does not fail to distinguish between false and real democracy – and that it does not ruin our entire economic system by making excessive demands due to lack of understanding and experience."

Within the next two decades, during the cold-dry period that is beginning – and is due to last, with the usual interruptions, at least for the rest of this century – we can expect that labor will continue to apply pressure for wage increases, decreased per-week work hours and increased representation in the councils of management.

In the most advanced countries, such as the United States, Britain, and the nations of Western Europe, the working classes will keep striking until they share in the ownership and management of the business world. There will be some anarchism until the laboring classes become part of an extended "middle class." The reality of doing business in a constrained economy will force a cooperative enterprise between management and labor, until perhaps, the familiar distinctions will disappear.

Judging by past activity in the revolutionary cold periods, the democratizing of business is inevitable.

"The problem," we are instructed by Wheeler, "is to expand democracy by voluntary means, preserving democratic institutions and laws while the expansion process is being achieved. Now, during the next few decades, this new and powerful class of voters, the laborers, must, in a sense, be absorbed into the middle class and be given middle-class concepts of free enterprise and democracy. While assuming greater responsibility, they must experience success in helping democracy work; or else, when it turns warm again and centralizing and socializing trends get under way once more, there will be nothing but stagnation and ruin ahead. If this happens, the next warm period will produce a despotism as catastrophic for modern civilizations as were the final despotisms of Greece and Rome.

"By the proper emphasis upon education in our schools and by the proper cooperation between capital and management on the one hand and labor on the other, such a catastrophe can be prevented. During the next few decades when both the middle class and labor are democratically minded is the time to stabilize our institutions – enriched by the contributions and cooperation of labor – to the end that they will not collapse in the warm periods to come."

Down through history, the people who had control of the government and the economic system have resented and feared the necessity of sharing their power with additional classes of society. Although the social revolution of the working class may appear threatening to the middle class from today's perspective, Wheeler assures us that "the conflict between management and labor contains no necessary threat to society and will not culminate in socialism or communism. When viewed in the light of historical ecology, it is only the next and expected step in the evolution of true democracy. The net result of the revolution will, in the end, be greater opportunity and freedom for all classes."

Civilizations, like people, seem to get sick every so often.

Some civilizations and cultures have become so sick that they have died or disappeared. By the time that happens, there is usually only a fraction of the original population left. That remnant wanders off and mingles with other societies — or else they are powerless to prevent other cultures from moving into their region and assuming control.

In some cases, the death of a civilization leaves the whole area so devastated and disintegrated that the people left there revert to primitive, semi-savage levels and remain there for quite some time. Eventually, though, a new society rises out of the ruins of the old.

Those of us who are living today are entering a cold-dry period and witnessing a time of revolution. Foresight and understanding will be needed by the civilized world if it is to survive the necessary changes without succumbing to catastrophe. No longer will nations be overrun by migrating hordes; however, as a result of wars in this century, the world has witnessed mass movements of peoples that far surpass the numbers of any historical migrations.

Out of the reshuffling and societal confusions will come a new epoch in history, beginning by 2000, bringing with it a renaissance, unprecedented prosperity, and world government. This collective rebirth will involve the great masses of the people participating in the economic and political structures to an extent unknown before in history.

As a consequence of these changes, Wheeler believed that the prevailing political structure will be neither fascism nor communism, but a purer, truer, more effective and complete democracy than has ever been known. Those of us who will be alive at the termination of this coming time of famine, revolution, depression and the collapse of the old civilization, will witness the advent of another Renaissance, a surge of renewed life force, a viable political and economic structure.

The turning point should come some time in the 1980s. Right now, according to the research of Raymond Wheeler, we are living at a time comparable to 1480, just before the advent of the great Renaissance of 1500.

What if the cycles should suddenly be altered and the next thirty or forty years should prove to be warm, rather than cold?

Even though the next twenty years are going to be very rough, a period of warmth would be the worst possible thing with our civilization as sick as it is right now.

Comparing Raymond Wheeler's detailed study of the rise and fall of civilizations to longtime weather trends, if we went through a long warm trend now, we would probably end up the way the Greek city-states did when they attempted state socialism – or we would probably sink into almost total destruction the way Rome did after she tried to dole out sustenance to the entire known world.

Socialistic trends develop during warm cycles, especially the hot drought periods in the one-hundred-year cycle. The revival of individual responsibility and an emphasis on free competition, private enterprise and personal freedoms always occur during cold times.

People are generally more ambitious and driven during cold times. They are more optimistic and much more willing to take chances. Cold times are times of democratic revival. New ideas and methods can be more freely introduced in the cold periods.

But it is not going to turn warm. It has definitely turned cold already, and it should remain so until at least the end of this century. However, a revival of democracy and individual responsibility is not assured.

First of all, democracy must be adjusted to the new age which emerges out of the ruin of the old civilization.

Secondly, there must be men and women with the energy and determination to create a democratic revival when nature has supplied them with the vitality and inclination to do so.

If too many people slump into an attitude of pessimism and indifference toward our societal welfare and maintain a sense of despair while the old world is dying, there will probably be enough of a socialistic foundation left over from the previous warm period to permit totalitarianism to engulf us before anyone realizes what is happening . . . and before the next warm period has scarcely begun.

Long-time antiwar activist Dave Dellinger has commented that in his estimation the Three Mile Island incident signaled the beginning of a new era:

"In nuclear power, we've got a gut issue which affects everybody, in many ways, even more dramatically than Vietnam did. It took a while for Vietnam to sneak up, but after Three Mile Island, everybody is worried; everybody is upset – whatever their politics or religion or lack of either.

"I only hope that when we do organize we don't fall into the narrow patterns that plagued the movement in the '60s – becoming one-dimensional, becoming single-issued, forgetting that there are many paths and that there is much richness to life, and that somehow or other we have to have heterogeneity and we also have to have unity – because we are all one."

At the end of one of these five-hundred-year rhythms civilization needs a thorough reorganization. In the past, each time one of these cycles evolved, civilization emerged from the chaos and confusion in much better condition, with a new unity and strength of purpose.

15

Shaping Destiny

A round 2040, perhaps a bit earlier, a heat climax will occur that will probably exceed the temperatures of the 1930s. This might well be the apex of the current one-thousand-year cycle.

After the heat climax, glaciers will begin to advance again, and the world's temperatures will fall until a cold climax is reached around 2500. At that time, the world will experience another upheaval as complete as that which terminated the Middle Ages and inaugurated our modern world.

"I have always insisted that the outlook for man is not fatalistic, integrated though he is with his environment and subject profoundly to climatic influences," Dr. Wheeler stated. "There is no excuse whatsoever for becoming an environmental determinist – at least of the kind known to the history of science."

Everything that happens in this world must have a reason. The science and philosophy of the past have given to humanity differing points of view regarding reasons for events. One world view supposes that the universe operates in accordance with blind, mechanical laws, that the forces of nature are physical (in the sense of material forces), based on matter as the ultimate reality.

"If this philosophy is carried out consistently to its natural conclusion, as certain philosophers and scientists of the past have done, there is no place for the mind in such a world; there is no place for human values; there is no place for God," Dr. Wheeler said. "The universe is a vast, meaningless machine, having no purpose, going nowhere . . . . The human organism, like everything else in the world, is but a mere machine, a robot, whose feelings, thoughts and longings have no more significance than the bumping of one atom into another. Human life has no more purpose, no more value, than a stone, among millions of other stones, clinging to the side of a vast mountain.

"The fact that most scientists will not carry such a view through to its logical conclusion, and that there have been but few philosophers down through history who were willing to do so – although they entertained a materialistic and mechanistic view of nature for everything outside of human affairs – is sufficient to prove the emptiness of the view itself."

Although the critical mind has not always found it easy to offer a substitute, scientists and philosophers who have provided an alternate view have outnumbered the first group several-to-one all through history. The second means of viewing the environment is the organic and idealistic view, as opposed to the mechanical and materialistic one.

The organic view maintains that the laws of nature are not wholly mechanistic. Predictability and regularity do not imply a fortuitous operation of mechanical forces. We are not machines. The universe is not a machine.

The term "material" has no meaning when applied to physical forces; the term "matter" has no meaning when applied to the world in which we live – or when applied to the human race. In fact, the term "physical" has no meaning other than a superficial and convenient one. It is merely a descriptive term which conveniently distinguishes certain types of phenomena – or certain types of events – from others just as the term "robin" points to a class of birds to be distinguished from "pheasants."

But if there were not something to the universe in addition to its separate parts, these parts would not be interrelated; there would be no whole; there would be just the parts.

In this sense the whole is oversummative or supersummative. It is more than the sum of its parts. Many different terms have been used to describe this "something more": organization, relations, integration, system, preestablished harmony, field property, plan, design, intelligence, world soul, God.

"Since the universe is a vast Unity, each part in it from the smallest to the largest, the simplest to the most complex is related to every other," Dr. Wheeler wrote. "This means that whatever it is, and whatever it does, each part has a function to carry out in the 'plan' of the whole."

According to modern science, no activity can transpire in the world, there can be no motion of any kind, unless nature as a whole obeys laws of equilibrium. Activities have direction, or they cannot occur. Thus, while activity is going on, the state of equilibrium is in the future, but the events that are now occurring are doing so with reference to that future state.

In other words, the conditioning factor – or at least one conditioning factor that is assumed to be necessary for the action – lies in the future of the events in question. The event is headed toward the goal of future equilibrium. The purpose of the event is the restoration of the system to equilibrium.

One could go further and show that, by definition, this equilibrium is an ideal state.

The goal is always ahead; it is never reached, but gives direction, always, to present events. Absolute, permanent equilibrium in the universe would mean the end of all activity. In human affairs that "direction" gives a purpose to the individual life and to collective living.

Thus it is that human behavior can follow the same ultimate laws as any other type of event in nature, without jeopardizing human values.

Human ideals are objectives of one kind or another, that, by definition, lie ahead of human action. If these ideals could be reached they would not be ideals. Like the condition of perfect equilibrium of all the physical forces in the universe, they are forever in the future; but that future is forever giving direction to what is happening now.

"It is neither elevating the atom nor degrading man to assume that every object in the universe obeys the same laws," Dr. Wheeler assures us, "for the status of each object is defined, not by the laws it obeys, but by its function, or purpose, in a system where every part obeys the same laws of the whole. The functions or purposes of the two may be vastly different under the same laws.

"The human being has intelligence, which the atom or the rain or the heat or the cold does not have. Intelligence has a place, a purpose, in the world. What better purpose could it have than that of trying to ascertain the meaning of life and of the universe as the abode of man? What better purpose could it have than that of searching for the truth?"

"Knowing that in the past the excess energy that the human race has possessed under certain climatic conditions has led to destructive aggressiveness, man can determine that that aggressiveness be expressed in a constructive manner, which will result in happiness rather than in suffering; in life rather than in death," says Dr. Wheeler. "There is nothing about climate that says, 'Thou shalt kill'. It merely has determined the energy level (aggressiveness) that, in his stupidity and ignorance, man has used for purposes of killing."

There is the possibility that we will eventually be able to create enough of an artificial climate in which to live to keep us from going to extremes under the influence of natural climate.

Such climatic control may allow us to minimize the effects of the various cycles. It may allow us to reduce the lethargy and fanaticism associated with the hot and dry epochs and eliminate the civil wars associated with the colder times.

By submitting to the gas laws, we built engines which were capable of carrying us around the world on land, sea and air.

By submitting to the laws of electricity, we provided light and heat, and instruments of communication, which could bring people of different continents together as if there were no time or space.

By submitting to the inevitable facts of health and disease, we have reduced infant mortality, prolonged life, conquered devastating plagues, enabled the lame to walk, the deaf to hear and the blind to see.

Why, then, should we not control our destiny in much greater ways — in part by a regulation of the climate in which we live — and rid the world of overambition and decadence, of tyranny and anarchy, of slavery and war?

An understanding of the effect of the weather cycles gives us the map of our cultural shifts. It should also be the map we use to control those cultural shifts.

Part Two

Practicing Creative Visualization:

Key to Future Freedom

16

Concentrating on the Future

In the December 1979 issue of *Science Digest,* Dr. Carl Rogers, a psychotherapist who has been credited with having created "client-centered therapy," dealt with the question of whether human abilities may be expanding.

Dr. Rogers states his fear that our culture is deteriorating and approaching collapse — whether through nuclear holocaust, the destruction of our bureaucratic institutions or some as yet unidentified threat. At the same time, he writes, he has begun to perceive how we as a species might survive such deterioration:

"I believe I am seeing exciting evidence of new characteristics some of which involve a fresh perspective on the evolving possibilities of individuals, groups, and communities. I think I am gaining a new vision of some of the developments in the human species which may enable it to live through the period of decay. Perhaps we are witnessing a period of expanding abilities in humankind."

The "new" characteristics of which Dr. Rogers writes may be among the most ancient of human abilities, and, indeed, he does go on to speculate that "our more primitive capability, our largely unused right brain, is beginning to function again as it so often does in less 'civilized societies'." Dr. Rogers states that he has begun to look with fresh vision upon an entire range of experiences that scientists had formerly disdained.

Dr. Rogers has begun to consider the possibility of all sorts of experiences, which in the past he had relegated to the amorphous areas of mysticism or which he had quickly dismissed as being ridiculous. Now he conceives of the inner world of the psyche as bearing potentially rich resources to be explored and utilized.

"Inner space," he conjectures, "may even be more important than outer space, and perhaps we can learn to live an important part of our lives in it.

"Perhaps we are entering a transitional stage of evolution similar to that of the first sea creatures who laboriously dragged themselves out of the swampy bogs to begin the difficult and complex task of living on land," Dr. Rogers theorizes. "Are we, too, evolving into new spaces? Will we discover new energies, new forces, new ways of being? Are we entering new worlds of psychic space, as well as the world of outer space? What is the future of the human spirit? To me these are tantalizing, but definitely hopeful, questions."

In Part Two of this book I will share a basic method whereby you might arrive at your own answers to whatever questions may have arisen as I explained the complex and chaotic contemporary events indicated by the weather cycles. This method – whether you choose to label it self-hypnosis, meditation or creative visualization – employs an altered state of consciousness as a key to open the door to the future.

An understanding of the historical and weather cycles is merely a beginning. As with any understanding of general events, the next question is where you as an individual fit in. Through creative visualization and the other techniques I am about to teach you, you can create your own future, your own destiny within the context of the upcoming cold-dry period and the changes the earth will soon face.

You might ask why you need to enter a state of trance or a kind of self-hypnosis in order to practice this method. The answer is that such a self-induced state of altered consciousness will enable you to develop a mental attitude of tranquility and thereby permit you to focus more sharply on the Maxwell-Wheeler weather cycles and your own future to chart more precisely a productive course for the future. These states are merely a vehicle for a more productive understanding of yourself.

Let me clarify that hypnosis is never something that a hypnotist does to anyone. Hypnosis is something that the subject does to him- or herself.

The trance state is always a product of the subject's own inclinations, not those of a hypnotist's will. Therefore, you can quite easily hypnotize yourself.

But you are afraid to enter a trance state, you say. Isn't there a danger that you might sleep on, impervious to smoke, fire or an alarm bell? And isn't it risky to be playing around with trance states in the first place?

Actually, you probably enter a very natural trance state several times a day without any obvious kind of induction procedure.

While sitting in front of your television set, watching your favorite show, your attention will be fully focused on the screen. Your conscious mind will be deeply absorbed. You will become oblivious to what is happening around you. You may mumble a response if someone speaks to you, but you really will not have heard a word.

Your little son may yank the cat's tail. You will hear nothing of the feline yowls of pain and protest.

Your teenaged daughter knows from experience that this is the best time to ask you for the car keys, and you obediently hand them over immediately upon her request.

For the duration of the program – or as long as it holds your complete attention – you will be intensely alert to every motion and sound emanating from the television set. At the same time, you may be unaware of everything else in your environment. You may even become virtually unaware of your own body sitting in the easy chair.

Think of the time the boss at the office gave you a particularly tough assignment, one at which you desperately did not wish to fail. After several days of hard work, the solution seemed near at last. You became totally involved in going over your notes and integrating them with the new data that had just become available to you.

As you more completely narrowed your attention on the facts and figures arrayed before you, all other sounds in the office became an unintelligible hum.

When someone asked if you wanted coffee and rolls, you didn't hear a word.

The telephone rang repeatedly at the desk next to yours. It could just as well have been ringing in a room across the street. Your conscious mind was fully absorbed in solving that stubborn case. You were motivated by the thought of seeing your boss's face light up with satisfaction and hearing her voice pronounce your promotion.

And remember that time when someone else was at the wheel of the automobile, and you were absently watching the telephone poles whiz by. You were surprised when your friend or spouse shook you back into a shared reality. You had spontaneously induced a state of self-hypnosis as you focused your attention out of the window and on the telephone poles. You no longer heard the car radio. You no longer responded to conversation. You were deep within your own thoughts, your inner reality.

If you possess these three traits you will be a good subject for self-hypnosis and creative visualization: (1) You must have the ability to focus your attention and to concentrate; (2) You must have an openness to new experiences; and (3) You must have a willingness to comply with suggestions.

I do not think it undue flattery to suggest that your very choice of this book as important reading matter and your very desire to change your future implies that you exhibit the three required traits for success.

An important word must be said here about expectations: Until they become accomplished practitioners of creative visualization, many people feel mildly relaxed, but they are puzzled when they find that they remain in touch with external reality, their conscious minds and their thoughts. Even under the guidance of a practiced hypnotist they may feel as though they are quite capable of resisting commands. They may declare that they feel alert and awake, and they may be convinced that they are not even hypnotized.

After working with hypnosis and with thousands of subjects over the past twenty years, I can assure you that even a light state of trance is deep enough to permit you to begin to change your life through creative visualization.

You see, contrary to what you might have previously believed, entering a trance state does not mean that you are surrendering control to another or blanking out your perceptions. A trance may actually give you total and complete control of your reality for the first time in your life. A trance is more like a daydream that heightens your perceptions and sharpens your command over both the magnitude and the minutiae of your existence.

Writing in the January 1983 issue of *Esquire* magazine, author Thomas B. Morgan told of his beneficial experiences with self-hypnosis in an article entitled "The Power of the Trance."

Morgan defines self-hypnosis and its successful applications in the following enthusiastic words:

". . . It is a temporary, self-managed altered state of consciousness that can make the resources of your brain and body and persona more responsive to your needs. Looked at another way, self-hypnosis is a natural phenomenon that helps you to follow your own suggestions, listen to your own admonitions and submit to your own commands (Isn't that what you always wanted to do?) just as the hypnotized subject in a one-to-one clinical session responds to the authority of a professional hypnotist during and after trance. In self-hypnosis, you are *both* subject and hypnotist. . . ."

The trance is truly not a "sleep" as you may have been led to believe by dramatizations of the process. If the fire alarm goes off, Morgan assures you that you will get out of your chair and walk to the nearest exit.

Trance, Morgan writes, is ". . . a *working* dream . . . a kind of business-like hyperconsciousness that lets you concentrate, really concentrate, on a matter of importance . . . and all under your control."

In this book, we are concentrating on the future, for we all agree that the future is a matter of great importance that we wish to control.

Part of the success of creative visualization will be my ability to convince you of its effectiveness. But before I get on with the actual business of showing you *how* it is done, I am going to quote an endorsement from Thomas B. Morgan:

"Think of it! No group sessions; no drugs, prescription or otherwise; no dope smoke; no hot tubs; no weekend retreats; no mantras, rock music, or voodoo paraphernalia; no hangovers or nightmares; no soy nuts or carob bars; no coin tossing, Rolfing, or biological backfeeding; and no deity, charismatics or Big Brothers. Self-hypnosis, folks, is cheap, healthy, painless and useful, and it travels well through time and space. Moreover, it feels good."

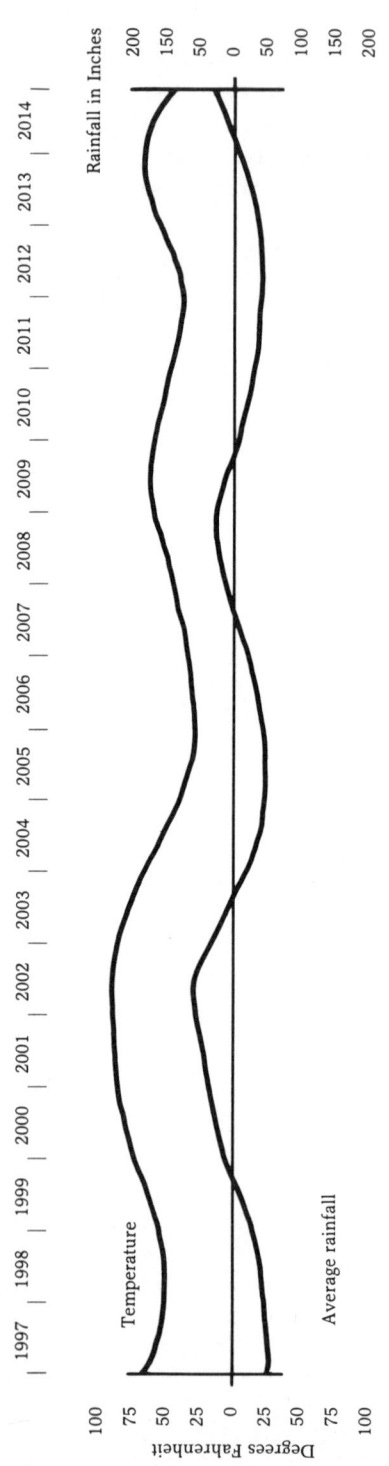

Forecast of Weather Trends
Based on Past Records

17

Breaking the Time Barrier

Is it really possible to see the future? Is it possible to move through Time to view scenes from the past and from other probable realities?

For the reader of this book, these questions take on several different gradations of meaning. An important secret has been revealed in the work of Maxwell and Wheeler: Time is nonlinear. Time moves in a spiral, a cycle, rather than a straight line.

Oh, yes, of course Time moves in a linear course in the material, Earthplane reality construct; but we are speaking now of a greater reality. We are speaking of the dimensions that truly shape the profound perimeters of what is real and what is unreal.

Can we, then, change the course of future events or is everything inexorably preordained?

It is perhaps not so much a question of our free will as it is a matter of what truly constitutes Time.

"In any attempt to bridge the domains of experience belonging to the spiritual and physical sides of our nature," wrote A.S. Eddington, "Time occupies the key position."

From the enriched perspective of this book, you can see that the concept of Time entertained by the general masses and the technologists is a naive one. An overwhelming number of us see Time as an absolute; however, the vast testimony of precognitive dreams has convinced many serious thinkers that certain men and women have occasionally broken loose from the evolved sensory pattern to receive a glimpse of the true order of the universe.

Dreams are paranormal phenomena with which everyone can identify. Only the most cynical deny the richness or the value of the dream experience.

Precognitive dreams may show us future possibilities or future actualities. They may indicate what *may happen* if we pursue a certain course of action, and they may show us a *precise event* which, seemingly, cannot be altered.

When you have viewed a future actuality — regardless of how many people tell you that you are mistaken — your "hunch" usually proves you to be absolutely correct. You have all had times when you knew that you were right in doing what you had to do.

What is it that occurs when one has truly glimpsed the future?

I have had precognitive dreams and visions of profound, as well as exceedingly mundane, occurrences. When I had such an experience, could I have *changed* the future event?

In my opinion, true foreknowledge of the future is known to some level of the subconscious. The level that is aware occasionally flashes a dramatic bit or a scene to the conscious mind in a dream or in a trance. The foreknowledge of the future is also founded on the knowledge of how the individual will use his or her freedom of choice.

In other words, the "future event" conditions the subconscious self. The level of the subconscious that "knows" the future does not condition the "future event." The transcendent element of self which knows what "will be" blends all Time into that moment of precognition.

For the conscious self, what is now the past was once the future. We do not look upon past events and feel that we acted without freedom of will. Why then should we look at the future and feel that those events are predetermined?

The fact that a level of psyche may know the future does not mean that the conscious self has no freedom of choice. Simply stated, if the future could be changed, it would not be the future. In a true precognitive experience when one perceives the future, he or she has glimpsed what will be and what, for a certain level of the subconscious, already exists.

There are, perhaps, five general types of precognitive experiences.

At the most elementary level is a subliminal precognition or the "hunch" that proves to be an accurate one. There is absolutely no slur intended in labeling this type of experience as "elementary." Some hunches have saved lives and established many giants of industry and commerce.

Next would come trivial precognition, which takes place only a short time before the actual occurrence of a rather important event.

Then, in the areas of full-blown, meaningful precognitions, which indicate a power of the mind not limited by Time and Space, there are beneficial, non-beneficial and detrimental precognitions.

In a beneficial premonition, I have observed, the transcendent level of self may over-dramatize a future event in such a way that it proves to be a warning that is acted upon by the conscious self's characteristic reaction to a crisis.

In the classic work, *An Experiment with Time,* J.W. Dunne provides many examples of his own precognitive dreams, which he recorded over a period of several years. He firmly believed in sleep and dreams as the prime openers of the subconscious, and he formulated a philosophy, which he called, "Serialism," to account for precognition.

In Dunne's view, Time was an "Eternal Now." All events that have ever occurred, that exist now or that will ever be, are everlastingly in existence. In our ordinary, conscious, waking state, he writes, our view is only of the present. In sleep, however, our view might be sufficiently enlarged to allow several glimpses of the future.

The philosophy of Serialism offers the challenge of bold and imaginative thinking. For example, in regard to *deja vu,* the sense of the already seen, Dunne suggests that this curious experience (which nearly everyone has had at one time or another) of "having been here before," is due to the stimulation of a partially remembered precognitive dream. When the conversation becomes familiar or the new location becomes suddenly recognizable, you simply remember a precognitive dream that had been driven back into the subconscious.

I have always loved St. Augustine's bemused evaluation of the nature of Time. "Time?" he puzzled. "What is it? If nobody asks me, I know. But if I am asked, I do not know!"

It soon becomes obvious that the conventional idea of Time existing as some sort of stream flowing along in one dimension is an inadequate one. In this view, the past does not exist: it is gone forever. The future does not exist because it has not yet happened. The only thing that exists is the present moment.

But the present does not really exist, either; for it is no sooner "now" than that "now" becomes part of the past. What was the future when you began to read this page was fleetingly the present and has already become the past by the time you will read the next word.

If the past completely ceased to exist, we should have no memory of it. Yet each of us has a large and a varied memory bank. Therefore, we know that the past must exist in *some* sense; not, perhaps, as a physical or material reality, but in some sphere of its own.

Similarly, the future must also exist in some way in a sphere of its own.

The key that you must come to possess is the knowledge that the subconscious does not differentiate between past, present and future, but is aware of all spheres of Time as part of the "Eternal Now."

At the same time, you must learn to distinguish between certain kinds of precognitive experiences and to identify them as part of the normal processes of the subconscious.

A woman dreams of coming down with measles and laughs it off. She did not succumb to the disease as a child, why should she as an adult?

In two days, she is in bed with the annoying rash covering her body.

Rather than judge this to be a prophetic dream, we might better regard the experience as an example of the subconscious mind being much more aware of the condition of the inner body than the conscious mind.

In other instances, as we have seen, a keen intellect and a great awareness of environment will enable one to make predictions. Those men and women who have become affluent due to such diverse activities as stockmarket juggling to hemline raising have gained their wealth because of their abilities to assess the preferences of a mass society in alignment with cycles of past human enterprises and endeavors.

The true power of prophecy rests not in some arcane and hidden knowledge, but within the transcendent self, which seems to be aware of events that belong in the realm of the future for the conscious self.

"Time is a condition created by the mind while we are on earth so that we can appreciate space – Time and Space being, in normal conditions, interlocked," the late British seer John Pendragon once told me.

"This also involves the intriguing and debatable question regarding fate and free will."

Most people seem to imagine that events that lie in what we term the future are "fixed" on a sort of moving belt that we call Time, and that Time moves the event out of the future into the so-called present and later into the so-called past. If they reflected for a moment, they would realize there is no such thing as the present. Utter the word "present" or "now," and even as you utter it, part of the word has vanished into the past, while the part yet to be uttered is still a fraction of a second in the future. Nobody can isolate a point in time and say, "This is the present."

It clearly seems, then, as Pendragon suggested, that Time has something to do with consciousness. Either an event has not happened yet or it has happened – at least that is how it seems while we are apparently naturally and normally "locked" in our bodies, never forgetting that we are *not* our bodies. The body is only a building to be occupied for a few score years.

If there is no present, how then is it that events are spaced out? If there is no present, then events must be either in the future or in the past. "Now" seems a very real thing to us. Nevertheless, even this illusive *now* has something strange about it. Sometimes now seems much longer than other times. The passage of Time is strangely elastic from the standpoint of the mind.

As a certain wit said, "When one is having a tooth drilled, a minute seems like an hour, but when one has one's sweetheart on one's knees, an hour seems like a minute!"

"It is difficult even to attempt to conjecture on the nature of Time, because one lacks an apt phraseology. Let me attempt to give my personal description," Pendragon stated.

"Let us suppose that one has a very long table, and at intervals of two or three inches a small object has been placed. First, for example, a button, then a matchbox, a pin, a bead and so on, until 50 or more objects have been spaced out down the table. Now the room is plunged into darkness.

"A person who has no knowledge of the objects on the table enters the darkened room. (In effect, he is born.) He is handed a very tiny, low-powered flashlight with a beam sufficient to illuminate, only *one object at a time.* He directs the beam on the first object – the button. The beam of light represents his consciousness. For a second he recognizes and appreciates the object that he has illuminated. Then he moves the beam on to the second object, and at the same time, the first one 'vanishes' into darkness again. Object one, by 'vanishing', has moved into the past. Meanwhile, object two, being illuminated, is in the present, whereas object three and all subsequent objects are in the future. Finally, after he has illuminated each object in turn, he reaches the last one, and his illumination – his consciousness in the 'beam sense' – goes out. (The moment of physical death.) Then somebody enters the room and switches on the big light over the table, and the examiner discovers that he can see *all* the objects at the same time. In short, his tiny beam of consciousness has been exchanged for a greatly enlarged one.

"Now that we have reached this comparison, we might add that a clairvoyant has a second tiny lamp which he can direct upon objects far down the line. The non-clairvoyant (if I may coin a word), on the other hand, has to direct his little beam on each object in strict rotation. No such limitation is imposed upon the clairvoyant, who can direct his second beam both backwards and forwards.

"Now I will attempt to give my personal opinions as to the nature of fate and free will.

"As I said earlier, there are persons who vaguely imagine that events that lie in what we term the future are all fixed on a sort of moving belt called Time, and all we can do is to sit back and wait for the belt to move the event into the present. To accept such a belief would be to embrace one of the enervating philosophies of the Orient.

"I may be wrong, but long experience has shown me – or appears to show me – that the stuff (I cannot find a more apt word) of the future is plastic. It can be molded by thought. In short, it is *psychoplastic.*

"If we hold a mind-picture for a long time, we tend to materialize it, especially if there is no doubt in our hearts and if we do not alter that picture. If we alter the picture or begin to doubt, we cannot bring what we desire out of the immaterial to the material. It is rather like getting a jelly to set. One must not stir it. The more powerful the thought and the sharper the picture, the more quickly we shall be able to materialize it.

"Let me add that this technique is indeed a two-edged weapon, for it will work for both good and evil. In the latter, it is a case of 'the thing I feared most has come upon me'."

The late Dr. Alexander Cannon told of a patient who was fearful of dying of a certain rare disease. She read everything that had been written about it, pondered her fear every day. In due time, she contracted the disease. She had clothed her thought in matter, but negatively so.

Thus it would seem that, to revert to the analogy of the moving belt called Time, it is possible to determine by voluntary action what sort of thing is to reach us on the belt. But we have to bear in mind that not one person in ten thousand makes a *deliberate technique* out of getting what they want. Life to them is mostly a patchwork of events. These persons are easier for the clairvoyant to "read."

Pendragon said that "Complex minds are much harder to delineate. It is often hard for the clairvoyant to determine the difference between the subject's thoughts at a given moment and an event which stands in the so-called future. Since it is my opinion it is also possible to mold one's future by deliberate thought (though I grant there may be limits to this, as I hope to show in a minute), it may be possible to change the nature of what the clairvoyant states lies in the future. In this case, the clairvoyant turns out to be 'wrong'.

"To put it another way, in certain instances it is possible to change the nature of what is seen by the clairvoyant, but only by deliberate action.

"I recall reading of a case recently in which a woman dreamed that she was in a car that had a tire blowout at a certain point on a cliff road. In the dream, the car plunged over the cliff. The day came when she was traveling in the car towards that point, but as the car neared the place where she had dreamed it would plunge over the cliff, the driver was ordered to slow down to three miles an hour. It was then that the car had the blowout — without falling to disaster over the cliff. Thus, it seems that what the clairvoyant 'sees' as a 'future event' may not necessarily be one, but the prediction is heeded and considered as a warning. My own opinion is that fate operates rather like this:

"A man may be fated to go from New York to San Francisco. This he is *fated* to do. There is no escape. He cannot go to any other destination. He must go to San Francisco.

"The element of free will enters into the matter with regard to the mode and route of his journey. He can fly directly from New York, or he can go by rail or by road. If he chooses road, he can go by car or even by bicycle or on foot. He can go by sea, via the Panama Canal. He can go north and then west via Canada and then south again, or he can sail due eastwards and approach San Francisco from the west. In the selection of a route he has choice, but in one thing he has no choice — his destination.

"I think that in one or two things we are fated, but that in a vast number we have free will. Whatever route we decided to choose, however, we only chose it as another means of getting to our fated destination.

"I have noticed, also, that those persons who govern nations are rather more fated than others. The same seems to apply to those whose lives are involved with the guidance or service of large numbers of other persons. Occultists always seem notoriously fated.

"I am deeply conscious that there are many possible answers to the age-old problem of fate and free will. I feel that it is always necessary to keep one's mind open. Anything in the nature of dogma must be avoided."

One of my own favorite analogies, which describes the true nature of Time, has a man riding on the rear platform of a train. He looks to the left and to the right. As the train chugs along, he is able to see a panorama of new scenes as they come into his view. As the train continues, these scenes fade into the distance and are lost to view. They have become his past.

However, the scenes do continue to exist after they have passed from the man's view, and they were in existence before he perceived them, even though he was only able to see them during the moments that they were his present.

At that same time, if another man were flying high above the train in an airplane, he would be able to see the train passenger's past and present, as well as future scenes, which lie beyond the man's limited ground-level view. All would exist for the man in the airplane as an "Eternal Now."

It is the task of one who wishes to create his or her own tomorrow to rise above the accepted limitations of consciousness and to abide, at least for a time, in the Eternal Now.

18

Eliminating Your Fear of the Future

Many of us at some time or other are troubled by phobic, fearful reactions to specific things or situations in our lives.

Under certain conditions these fears may have become so powerful that they inhibited or restricted our life severely. In some instances these phobias have crippled us and prevented us from complete development of ourselves or from achieving total fulfillment.

Some people have a phobic response to the future. The very thought of facing tomorrow with its changes, its alterations, its threats and its transitions strikes unreasoning fear in the very fibre of their being.

Some people fear tomorrow because of a basic lack of confidence in their ability to handle encounters with strange, new challenges. The very idea that the Old World is dying, that the world that they once knew is deteriorating all around them, fills them with such fear that they cannot appreciate the true promise of what is being born.

Here is an exercise that you might use to help you eliminate your fear of tomorrow.

Imagine that you are lying on a blanket on a beautiful stretch of beach. You are lying in the sun, or in the shade, whichever you prefer.

You are listening to the sounds of the ocean, the rhythmic sound of the waves as they lap against the shore. You are listening to the same restful lullaby that Mother Ocean has been singing to men and to women for thousands and thousands of years.

As you listen to that restful lullaby, it is singing to you of peace and tranquility. It is eliminating any fears, apprehensions and tensions that you may have about facing the future.

As you relax, nothing will disturb you. Nothing will distress you. Nothing will molest or bother you in any way.

You know that you have nothing to fear. Nothing can harm you. As you listen to the sound of the ocean waves, you feel all tensions, all fears leaving your body.

The sound of the waves helps you to become more and more relaxed. With every breath that you take you find yourself feeling better. You must permit your body to relax so that you may rise to higher states of consciousness where no fear exists. Your body must relax so that the *real you* may rise higher and higher to greater states of awareness.

You are feeling the beautiful energy of tranquility, peace and love entering your feet, and you feel every muscle in your feet relaxing.

That beautiful energy of tranquility, peace and love moves up your legs into your ankles, your calves, your knees, your thighs; and you feel every muscle in your ankles, your calves, your knees, and your thighs relaxing, relaxing, relaxing.

If you should hear any sound at all — a slamming door, a honking horn, a shouting voice — that sound will not disturb you. That sound will help you to relax even more.

Nothing will disturb you. Nothing will distress you in any way. Nothing will cause you fear or apprehension.

Now that beautiful energy of tranquility, peace and love is moving up to your hips, your stomach, your back; and you feel every muscle in your hips, your stomach, your back relaxing, relaxing, relaxing.

With every breath that you take you find that your body is becoming more and more relaxed. You are less and less fearful about the future.

The beautiful energy of tranquility, peace and love enters your chest, your shoulders, your arms, even your fingers; and you feel every muscle in your chest, your shoulders, your arms and your fingers relaxing, relaxing, relaxing.

With every breath that you take you find that you are becoming more and more relaxed. Every part of your body is becoming free of tensions, free of worry, free of fear.

The beautiful energy of tranquility, peace and love moves into your neck, your face, the very top of your head; and you feel every muscle in your neck, your face, and the very top of your head relaxing, relaxing, relaxing.

Your body is now relaxed, but your mind, your True Self is very aware.

Now you are considering your fear of the future. You will be able to study it, analyze it, without experiencing the tension, the discomfort that normally comes upon you.

Recall as totally as you can the emotions and physical responses that flow through you and constrict your brain and your body when you think of the future. Recall as completely as you can the quickening of the heart, the increase of the breath, the onset of heavy perspiration.

Remember a recent time in which you experienced a confrontation with your fear of the future. Go back to that moment; try to see it in your mind's eye as precisely as if it were happening right now. You will be able to do so without any tension, without any stress.

Try to recall what it was that first triggered your phobic response. Was it someone discussing a situation about the future in which you would have to confront your fear? Was it merely a reference to the subject matter of the future that brought about your discomfort? Or did you actually have a pre-vision of the fear itself?

After you felt the first tremor of fear, what did you do to make the feeling increase? If there were others present, what did they do to make your fear increase?

Was there a particular place in your body where you actually seemed to feel the tension and fear? What did you do then to make the feeling increase? If there were others present, what did they do to make your fear increase?

Was there a particular place in your body where you actually seemed to feel the tension and fear more than any other? Did you react most by trembling, feeling dizzy, or by feeling nauseated? Reflect for a moment on exactly which part of your body reacted most to the phobia.

Reflect on your body in such a manner so that you can focus on why you respond more in one part of your body than any other.

Begin to fantasize in a free associative manner. Did something connected with your fear of the future once become localized in that part of your body? Did something strike you there, burn you there, bite you there, crush you there?

Continue to free associate in such a manner. Where were you when the incident occurred? See yourself in an environment. See yourself suffering the trauma – whatever it may have been.

Now imagine that you can clearly see the time in which this trauma first occurred. See yourself as you appeared at that time. See the other people with whom you might have been intimately involved in that experience.

Focus again on the exact time reference of the original trauma.

You will be detached, but you will know strong emotional ties to that expression of discomfort. You will observe the event *only* for the purpose of freeing yourself from the fear that inhibits you today. You will observe the trauma *only* for the purpose of impressing upon all levels of your consciousness that the reason for the terrible fear that restricts you is a thing that you can conquer, that you can dissipate.

Impress on all levels of your consciousness, all aspects of your awareness, that your feelings of crippling fear toward the future are unnecessary.

Impress on all levels of your consciousness, all levels of your awareness, that you need not ever experience that fear again.

Impress on all levels of your consciousness, all aspects of your awareness, that your fear of the future is removed.

Understand that the fear and all of its consequences were the stuff of doubts and apprehensions.

One Minute a Day to Banish Fear of the Future

Remember always that you are a creator. What you *think*, you *create* on some level of consciousness, on some vibratory plane. Where your *attention* is, there *you* are. What you *wish*, you will *become*. What you *meditate upon*, you *will be*.

Therefore, rather than giving attention to your fear, rather than nurturing your apprehension, give your attention to your higher self for one minute a day, and you will receive so much powerful energy and bring so much good into your life that you will banish all fear of the future!

If for just one minute each day you spend just sixty seconds visualizing the most powerful energy in the universe moving into your body/mind . . . if you will spend just that brief time in your daily schedule to fix your attention on the harmonizing and the balancing of your body/mind . . . if you will spend one minute turning on your inner-light switch, you can control your reality and have no fear of the future ever again!

Dealing with a Negative Prediction of the Future

If you have received a prediction through a prophetic dream or vision that has warned you against a particular course of action, you must understand that the act of receiving that premonition does not mean that the adverse situation *must* take place.

You should interpret such a premonition as the mechanism of bringing the matter to your attention so that you can avoid any unfavorable action.

Remember, as was stated earlier, a negative premonition can simply be your inner self's awareness of the reality of time. It is using this awareness to warn you of an impending problem. It is then up to you to use your own free will to make the situation what you want it to be.

19

Using Your Dreams and Visions to Fashion a Better Future

I learned to control my dreams when I was twelve or thirteen years old. I remember that it happened in one of those childhood nightmares that everyone seems to have — one of those in which you can't run, you can't pull the trigger of the gun, and the monster just keeps getting closer, eager to tear you apart.

Then, within the frightening dream, a realization dawned upon me: "Hey, this is all going on inside of my own head! There is no need for me to be frightened. There is no need for me not to be in control of the situation!"

It was as if I had decided to step out of the dream for a bit to assume the assertive role of the Dream Director. I called things to a sudden halt. I commanded the monster and a nasty assortment of villains to stop right where they stood.

All the wicked agents of fear conceded that the dream truly did belong to me.

I next proceeded to dictate the terms of that, and any future dream: "From now on, when I pull the trigger of a gun, the gun will fire. Understand? It's just a dream, anyway, and you won't really be hurt.

"And when I want to run, there will be no more of this running-in-place, unable to move.

"And when I need to fight, I'll be a superman. No more of this ineffectual thrashing about."

All the monsters agreed. They would obey. They were, after all, creatures of my own invention or attraction. They could not really be hurt. They truly were the stuff of which dreams were made.

From that long-ago night onward, I have been able to control my dreams. I can stop them, start them, continue them.

My dreams have served as marvelous therapeutic devices. They have also assisted me in memorizing texts, speeches, and lessons.

Since earliest childhood, I have had an astonishingly easy access to other states of consciousness, to the door that opens between dimensions. I have never had the need to indulge in marijuana or any of the more powerful mind-altering drugs. I seem to have access within me to far greater experiences than drugs could ever supply. I must agree with the Yogis that drug-induced experiences are but reflections of the true inner adventures achieved through the resources that already exist within us.

Developing Control of Your Dreams

How can I teach you to develop dream control?

First of all, *believe* that if I was able to achieve such control, so can you.

You will have to apply yourself, however. I cannot simply present you with one or two magic words to utter.

Dream control involves an effort of the will. But I can promise you that the rewards that may be reaped by such an effort are nearly inestimable in terms of their long range value to you as a person.

As you are falling asleep, suggest to yourself that you have the ability to develop full mastery of your dream states. If you have been suffering from nightmares, you must use an effort of will to separate yourself from the scenario of terror.

Understand that nightmares transpire within the theater of your own mind. Demand that you be given the control of your own inner machinery.

Control of your dreams and your inner life helps you to establish an aura of confidence and of control toward your waking life and your external environment. The *modus operandi* of one who will create a positive tomorrow most emphatically includes a positive assertiveness toward the outside world.

Understand that as I write such words, I am also reminding you of balance, the great metaphysical law. I am not encouraging you to exercise a tyrannical approach toward the lives of those around you. But I am insisting that you assume an attitude of confidence toward any situation in which you may find yourself.

Remember the old metaphysical maxim that you have heard so often: "As above, so below."

There is yet another maxim that relates to dream control: "As within, so without."

If you have achieved true self-mastery within, your task of molding the external world to your satisfaction will be so much more easily attained.

Of course, we must have the wisdom to know the difference between those external situations that may be malleable to our will and those that are set before us as unalterable cosmic testing devices.

Perhaps this attitude is best personified by the Native American concept of becoming a spiritual warrior, balancing the terror of being human with the wonder of being human.

Dream-teachings, visions of guidance, and inspirations for service to others are all best attained by sincere and respectful journeys into the Silence of meditation.

The essence of Silence is the power of Light and an unconditional love of the Earth. Pulsating deep within such light and such love is the essence of the Source of All-That-Is.

Preparing for a Vision

On the day when you want to have a particularly meaningful dream, it is wisest to make a direct request for the experience immediately upon arising. With your first consciousness and prayerful activity, begin to make a positive affirmation that your vision will be achieved.

Then, from time to time throughout the day, still yourself, if even for a moment, and give recognition to the Source that exists above you and which exists also within you.

Visualize the Source as the eternally powerful energy that ignites the golden flame that burns within you. The more profoundly that you can experience this connection, the greater the results of your vison.

Visualizing the Source of All-That-Is

Although we realize that the force that controls all is energy, it does aid us in achieving the transfer if we visualize It as an individualized presence.

Some still prefer the image of a loving Father or Mother. Others focus upon the image of a glowing Light Being.

Since we humans seem to communicate more effectively with images that most resemble us, I always encourage my students to develop a personal idea of a loving intelligence that is ready to answer their every call, that is willing to grant every request that is for their good and their growth.

It is truly important that you visualize and attempt to feel the reality of that individualized presence above you. Know that It is connected to you by a ray of light, a stream of energy that flows into your body.

Several times a day before seeking a profound vision, give your attention to the image you have chosen and send your love to that presence. Just remember that the summoning of a vision must always be as the result of a balanced desire.

Remembering Dream Teachings

There may be occasions when you will awaken in the night and know that you have been receiving dream teachings. You may feel distressed when you become aware that you have been unable to retain the full importance and meaning of the teachings.

Call to your inner self and ask that you be allowed to recover the full understanding of the message. Ask that you again receive the full power of the vision or the teaching which has just been entrusted to you.

Do not permit yourself to become angry or frustrated for having permitted the lesson to have become lost to your waking consciousness.

If you should not be able to recall the lesson on that particular evening, go back to sleep with the resolution that you shall reclaim it on the next night.

Charge yourself to bring back the vital substance of the dream teachings that you shall receive anew.

Banishing Disturbing Dream Images

Even after you have developed dream control, you may, from time to time, receive disturbing dream images about certain individuals or about people in general. It is not good to harbor this vague, but often troublesome, dream residue.

When you arise and go about your daily tasks, visualize the violet light of transmutation upon everyone you meet. Soon, only positive thoughts about all individuals will command your attention.

If you should awaken some evening and feel that you have been bombarded with negativity while you were open to receive a vision or a dream teaching, deal with the chaotic energy in this manner:

Visualize your head filled with a blazing white light. Imagine that you are focusing the energy of the Sun through your brain.

Conceive of the room becoming so bright that you can hardly keep your eyes open.

Expand the light to shine beyond your bedroom. See it shining upon your neighborhood, your city, your nation, your world. Then visualize yourself suspended in space watching your brilliant light touching the universe.

See that your heart has become a golden sun, then expand the light again to fill the room, the neighborhood, the city, the nation, the world, until it touches the universe.

Now feel that your body has turned to metallic gold. You have converted the lead of your body into the finest quality gold.

As a golden being, hold in your mind a request for the kind of vision or teaching which you feel that you most require for your good and your growth. Continue to hold that request in your mind until you fall asleep again.

20

Exploring a Future Lifetime

I believe that it is important for the expanded human to explore the Soul memories of his or her past lives. The less-aware may take the stance that they are having enough trouble with their present existences and that there could be little to gain from knowledge of prior life experiences, but I am convinced that one should desire to seek the balance of past life lessons.

My position is that knowledge of past lives is a form of awareness that can aid one in creating a more complete present-life existence, which, in turn, will help to shape a more positive, productive, peaceful future.

It has now become tedious for me to argue whether past-life recall is pure fantasy or the actual memory of a prior existence. What is important is that, time and time again, I have witnessed men and women obtaining a definite and profound release from a present pain or phobia by reliving the origin of their problems in some real or alleged former existence. Whether that is because of past life therapy or because of the belief in past life therapy is immaterial. It works.

I believe that we should accept full responsibility for our actions. If you should be troubled by a phobic response to any aspect of your life, it is important that you determine the cause of your phobia. If you have spent several contemplative – but unsuccessful – moments seeking the cause of your problem in your present life experience, you should turn back the pages of your past-life Soul memories.

When you relive what may be a past life, you become capable of accepting responsibility for a past action that may have been performed in another lifetime. Once you have made the transfer of responsibility to the present life and recognized that the fault lies in a time far removed from current concerns, you will be able to deal with the matter without embarrassment or shame.

Knowledge of past lives is but another form of the extended awareness that must by synonymous with enlightenment.

Such extended awareness can bring you much more than past-life memories – even more than the resolution of specific current problems. By exploring prior-life experiences, you may truly come to know yourself and to recall physical and mental skills that you may have mastered in other lifetimes. You may discover talents that can bring greater creativity to your present life. You may relearn how to become more efficient in the performance of daily tasks.

Interestingly, the extended awareness that you receive from past life memories will serve to enhance all the pleasures that you derive through your senses in your present life. Your sight, your hearing, your touch, your smell, your taste will all become keener. You will be capable of detecting subtleties that you've never before noticed. You will achieve a deeper insight into the actions of others, and you will gain a greater control of your life and yourself.

Just be cautious that you do not use your psychic tools simply to build a large ego for yourself. Don't waste precious moments "remembering" your lifetimes as great and illustrious historical personages. Put the past to work in order to construct a brighter, more fulfilling future.

It is easier to face the future once you have come to terms with the past. And by remaining truthful with yourself about the actual reality of your past, you will have a much better chance of building a more positive tomorrow.

Statue Projection Exercise to the Past

Practice a steady, deep breathing technique to place yourself in a state of reverie and receptivity.

Visualize yourself walking through a great and magnificent temple in some other dimension of being. This temple is dedicated to artistic representations of the Soul and its various expressions throughout history. As you turn a corner, you suddenly confront a statue of yourself as you looked in an important past-life experience.

Imagine the statue before you. Even though the figure may not greatly resemble you in your present-life experience, you are certain beyond all doubt that it is really you.

Of what material has the statue been made?

How large is the statue?

In what pose has the statue been fashioned? What is the figure doing?

Is the figure male or female?

From what you can assume, in what field of thought, endeavor, or accomplishment did the figure excel?

Now study the statue carefully. Feel yourself becoming one with the statue. Feel yourself breathing life and warmth into the statue. See yourself reliving the important events of that lifetime that resulted in a statue being made in your likeness.

In what country or place and in what historical time did you live?

What was your greatest ambition in that lifetime? What did you want most to accomplish?

Now visualize scenes of conflict, scenes of strife. See if you sense or perceive anyone from your present-life experiences striving against you in that lifetime. If you recognize anyone at all, take a few moments to contemplate what lesson you see here that can help you resolve some aspect of your present-life experience.

Now see if you sense or perceive anyone from your present-life experience who is championing you, supporting you, working with you in those scenes of strife and chaos. If you recognize anyone at all, take a few moments to contemplate why you have come together again in your current lifetime.

Scan that lifetime and visualize the events of greatest conflict. After you have reflected upon these situations for a few moments, imagine the events and occasions of your greatest triumphs.

Did you achieve your goal in that lifetime?

How did you die?

What was the most important lesson that you learned from that lifetime?

What situation would you most like to redo in that lifetime? What patterns of behavior would you least wish to replicate?

The survival of the Essential Self and the reality of other lives became real for me on August 23, 1947, when, as a boy of eleven, I died – or, for a time, seemed to die – as the result of a terrible accident.

I can profoundly recall the sensation of soaring suddenly high above the Iowa field where a boy lay crushed and bleeding. I felt very detached from him. I seemed only dimly aware of our association. I had become my essence, an orangish-colored ball, intent only on soaring toward a brilliant light. I felt blissfully euphoric, and I gloried in a marvelous sense of Oneness with All-That-Is.

From time to time, I would be shown *something* that I can now best remember as a kind of great tapestry of life, which somehow demonstrated the order and the rightness of existence.

I was in and out of my body during the desperate 140-mile run to a hospital in Des Moines where my physical life might be saved. Just before surgery was to begin, I came back to the body with such force that I sat up, shouted, and pushed an intern off-balance. It took the words of a Roman Catholic sister to calm me until the anesthesia could take effect.

Later, during my recovery period, the sisters knew that I had been "somewhere" and that I had seen "something." They would question me about my experience as a spirit traveling between two worlds.

Those discussions marked the beginning of my life's work of testifying that the human spirit-essence does survive physical death, that there is an existence that transcends the material realm. I have never considered myself "chosen" or "special," but I have always regarded myself as having been blessed with an experience that could translate into knowing that which others had to accept on faith alone.

When you begin to explore your experiences of altered states of consciousness even more extensively, it will be useful to you to be mindful of the "Hidden Observer," that ever-alert, constantly watchful facet of the Essential Self.

Recently, I worked with a woman in her sixties who had exceedingly firm mental blocks against reliving a childhood trauma. She had been to a succession of therapists and psychologists without achieving a breakthrough of any kind.

I began to speak to that within her which was basic to her survival as a sovereign entity. I asked to make contact with her Essential Self, the part of her that was always listening, always aware, always protecting her most vulnerable areas. Once I had proven my goodwill to that portion of her inner-self, we were able to travel together meaningfully to root out the negativity of that prior experience and to establish a purposeful future.

Dr. Ernest R. Hilgard discovered the Hidden Observer when he was about to demonstrate the power of hypnotic suggestion by slapping two wooden blocks together beside the ear of a student whom he had just "made" deaf.

Bang! Bang! The student made no response to the loud noises beside his ear, nor did he reply to any questions put to him by the hypnotist. Here, the hypnotist announced, was proof of altered-states over senses.

But, one of the students wondered aloud, might not there be some part of the "deaf" subject that might be aware of what was going on around him. After all, the man was not *really* deaf. There was really nothing wrong with his hearing.

The hypnotist had to agree. "Although I have suggested that you are hypnotically deaf," he said to his subject, "if there is some part of you that is hearing my voice and processing information, raise the index finger of your right hand to signal that this is so."

The index finger rose, and the subject spoke up: "Please, sir, let me hear you again so that you may tell me what you did. I felt an uncontrollable impulse to raise the index finger on my right hand, and I want to know why."

The hypnotist awakened the subject by the prearranged signal of a touch on his right shoulder; but without fully explaining what had occurred, he suggested that when he placed his hand on the subject's arm, he would be in communication with a hidden part of the mind.

When this had been accomplished, the hypnotist heard the subject telling him how many times he had slapped the boards beside his ear, repeating the questions raised to the members of the class, and restating the command that had caused his index finger to rise.

It was such a demonstration that clearly indicated to Dr. Hilgard, emeritus professor of psychology and education at Stanford University, the fact that ". . . a hypnotized subject who is oblivious to a source of stimulation . . . may nevertheless register the information. Further, he may understand it to the extent that, under appropriate circumstances, what was unknown to him can be uncovered and talked about."

Dr. Hilgard had encountered what he came to call, "The Hidden Observer," that part of a hypnotized subject that can give information not available to the hypnotized self. Awareness of such an ever-watchful, constantly alert segment of the self is of great importance to those who practice creative visualization and to those who might wish to add regression to the tool kit by which they build a more complete meaning of reality.

Writing in the January 1978 issue of *Human Nature,* Dr. Hilgard states that numerous experiments with the Hidden Observer, together with his findings on amnesia, automatic writing, age regression and hallucination, ". . . indicate the kind of vertical split common in hypnosis between what the hypnotized part experiences and what can be recovered from a parallel mental process that has been registering and storing additional information . . ."

Dr. Hilgard reminds us that the mystical or ecstatic view of consciousness as the mode of aesthetic sensitivity is valid, but incomplete. Consciousness also is the active "agent, planner and controller," for it is only through consciousness that we can visualize our goals and formulate images of our future.

For those who are both mystical and practical, the two modes of consciousness – the aesthetic and the active – may be entirely compatible. We may, indeed, go to the "mountaintop" to gain our inspiration and our mystical experience, then return to the valley of physical reality and minister to the sick, build bridges and teach others of the balanced life.

Most hypnotic behavior has to do with either the enhancement or the inhibition of normal control processes. It should be noted, however, that the normal control processes outside of hypnosis are more fragmented and much less unified than most people believe to be the case.

Dr. Hilgard tells us that while it is true that there are many diverse mental controls functioning within us, not all are active at once.

"At any one time, they are arranged in a kind of preferential order, so that some dominant control system has access to behavior, while other available control systems are in abeyance. Their position in the order changes as demands upon the person change . . . if it were not for some sort of preferential order, any triggered impulse might lead to a spasm of inchoate activity. Preferential control represents the normal manner in which our thoughts activate what we do, what we experience consciously, and what we keep in reserve for another occasion."

The order of preference, then, Dr. Hilgard advises us, becomes modified under hypnosis. And some cognitive systems – even when they are not functioning in consciousness – "continue to register and process incoming information." Moreover, the psychologist concludes, "When such a system is released from inhibition, consciousness uses this information as though it had been conscious all along. This is . . . the laboratory picture when the hidden observer is brought to light."

Such research as Dr. Hilgard's underscores aspects of responsibility that the casual practitioner of altered states explorations may not have considered carefully enough. One should always be cautious about extraneous verbal stimuli when working with altered states of consciousness. Because of the Hidden Observer, the environment that is created for a subject should be as conducive to a positive inner-journey as is possible to create.

Exploring a Future Lifetime

When my wife and I were working one-on-one with clients in daily regression sessions, we found it exceedingly effective to focus on a particular past life that may have been directly responsible for the troublesome imbalance – the phobia, guilt, compulsion, illness, whatever – of the subject's present-life experience. We were always distressed to encounter men and women who had been tormented by their maladjusted lives, men and women who had been desperately consulting psychologists, psychiatrists and medical doctors for years, with little or no progress made toward easing their pain.

Again and again in so many cases all we needed was one session with a subject in order to enable him or her to see that they had been unknowingly permitting unconscious memories of a prior existence to ruin the chances of establishing a fruitful relationship or a productive life. What was required was helping the client recognize the lessons that had been left unlearned from that other time and to assist him or her to begin to use the proper mental tools to make their present life truly workable.

In other experiments we discovered that effective therapy and numerous useful insights could also be achieved by projecting a subject into a future lifetime. Through this a meaningful dialogue could be established between a future self and the present self.

Use *any* of the relaxation techniques that may have been successful for you in previous experiments in creative visualization.

Once the body has been relaxed as deeply and completely as possible, permit the Real You to escape from its physical structure.

Don't worry. Your spirit – the *Real You* – will always return to your body, but for now you are free to soar into the future, totally liberated of time and space.

A swirling purple mist is moving all around you; you begin to move higher and higher, higher and higher.

You seem to be floating through space, moving gently through space, moving through all of time.

Time itself seems to be like a spiral moving around you, a spiral never ending, never beginning, never ending, never beginning.

You know that you have the ability to move forward through time and to see a future life that you need to know about for your good and your growth. A future life that may tell you very much about your present life.

Ahead of you, suspended in space, is a great golden door. And you know that when you step through that door you will be able to explore an important future lifetime.

You will be able to see the reasons why your soul chose the parents, the brothers or sisters, the friends, the mate, the nationality, the race, the sex, the talents, the occupation of that future time.

You will see the soul-chosen purpose for the agonies, troubles, pains, and griefs that will enter that future life.

The door is opening, and you step inside . . . .

You see yourself as you were when you were a child in that life.

If it is for your good and your growth, you are able to know what country you are living in – as you would understand it today – and what period of time you are living in – as you would understand it today.

You see the color of your eyes, your hair, your skin. You see clearly what sex you are.

Now see your body unclothed. See if you have any scars, birthmarks or other peculiar characteristics that are visible on your naked body.

Now you are clothed. See yourself in characteristic clothing for that future time. See clearly what is on your feet.

A man and a woman are now approaching you. Look at their eyes. It is the man and woman who are your *father and mother* in *that* life.

Understand what kind of relationship you have with them. Do they love you? Understand you? Reject you?

And now, for your good and your growth look at their eyes and see if either of them are with you in your present-life experience and have rejoined you in that future time to complete work left unfinished. . .to master a lesson left unlearned.

Someone else is approaching you, and you see that it is a brother or a sister with whom you are very close. Look at this person's eyes.

This is a brother or sister who loves you and supports you.

This is a person who is always there whenever you need help.

And now, looking into these eyes, for your good and your growth, see if that beloved brother or sister is with you in your present life, and has rejoined you in that future time to complete work left undone, to finish a lesson left unlearned.

Now, from that same future life someone else is approaching you in the home that you share with your parents in that lifetime.

It is a brother or a sister with whom you have rivalry and conflict. Look at the *eyes*.

This is one who seems to be undermining you in your relationship with your parents and with others.

Look into the eyes and see if you will ever resolve your conflict with this person.

Look into the eyes and see if this brother or sister is with you in your present life in any way.

See if that brother or sister came with you in that future time to complete work left undone, a lesson left unrealized.

Now, in that same future lifetime, scan the vibration of any other relative or family member — an uncle, a grandparent, a cousin — and see if any relative or family member from that time is with you in your present life.

In that same future lifetime you are growing older, moving into young adulthood, and you see yourself performing some favorite activity, a game, a sport, a hobby, that becomes so very much a part of your life.

You see yourself performing that activity, and you understand how it will become impressed on your future life pattern.

You are now beginning to see clearly and to understand what work you will do in that life. . .how you will provide for yourself or for others. . .how you will spend your days.

Someone is approaching you from that work situation. Look into the eyes.

This may be someone who is your employer, your boss, your overseer.

This may be someone who is your employee.

But this is someone with whom you will interact closely at your work.

For your good and your growth, look at the eyes; see if this person is with you in your present-life experience and has rejoined you to complete work left undone, to learn a lesson left unaccomplished.

As you move away from your work situation, you are beginning to feel the vibrations of love moving all around you. You are aware of someone standing there, to your left, standing there in the shadows.

You are feeling love – warm, peaceful sensations of love – moving all around you, as you realize that standing there in the shadows is the person whom you will love most in that lifetime.

Look at the eyes. Feel the love flowing toward you from those beautiful eyes of your beloved.

Look at the smile of recognition on those lips as the beloved one sees you and begins to move toward you.

Now, for your good and your growth, look at the eyes. See if this beloved one is with you in your present-life experience.

See if you have come together again to work out a task left incomplete, a lesson left unlearned.

You are growing older in that life. See now the one whom you will marry in that life. Will it be the one you loved most? Or will that beloved one be taken from you by death . . . or other circumstances?

If the one you see before you now is not the one you loved most, then, looking at the eyes, see for your good and your growth the person you *will* marry. And see if that person is with you in your present life.

If you have children in that future life, see them now. See their eyes looking up at you. Feel their little hands on your fingers. Feel the love flowing from them.

Now see scenes from that future life that you need to remember for your proper soul evolution.

See scenes that will help you in your present-life experience.

These are scenes you need to remember, but you will see them in a detached manner. You will feel neither guilt nor shame. You will feel neither pride nor ego pleasure. You will understand *why* they will happen.

You will understand these acts so that your Soul may grow and gain.

And now, for your good and your growth, witness the moment of your death in that life.

Perhaps you will not be ready for death . . . perhaps you will fight against it . . . curse it. But understand why your soul will withdraw its energy at that time.

See who is with you at that last moment. Is it the one you loved most? Your family? Your children? Or . . . are you all alone? Do you face that last moment all alone?

You see clearly why you had to come again to put on the fleshly clothes of Earth in a future life.

You see why certain people are with you now, and why they will rejoin you to complete work left undone, to master a lesson left unlearned.

You see and understand clearly what you are to do in your present life that will most aid you to accomplish your mission.

You are filled with a wonderful sense of well-being for now you know what you must do. You see clearly what you must do to fulfill totally your true mission in life. You no longer feel sensations of frustration and anxiety.

Now you *know*. You know why you came to Earth, why you chose to put on the clothes of Earth, why you chose to assume the Karmic vibrations of this planet.

You are beginning to awaken, feeling very, very good . . . very, very positive.

You are filled with a beautiful, glowing sense of your mission.

You are filled with the positive knowledge that you will be able to accomplish so much toward your true mission now that you are filled with awareness of your future lifetime.

Now you understand much more of the great pattern of your total life experience.

Awaken with positive feelings of love, wisdom, and knowledge. Awaken feeling very, very good in the body, mind, and spirit. Awaken feeling better than you have felt in weeks, in months, in years. Awaken filled with love, filled with knowledge.

21

The Native American and Huna Power Systems

Our Native American priests, the Medicine Men and Women of the tribes on the North American continent, together with the Kahuna on the Hawaiian Islands, for centuries practiced a system of magic that was so powerful that it enabled them to control the winds and the weather, to foresee the future and sometimes to change the future. They had the ability to heal the sick instantly, to walk over hot lava and hot coals, to read minds, to send and receive telepathic thoughts – and sometimes it is said, even to pray their enemies to death. There is no question in my mind that these native priests were masters of creative visualization.

Huna was the most powerful religious system in the Polynesian Islands before the introduction of Christianity. Western culture could not compete with the Kahuna priest on his own terms, so it instigated a program of limiting his practice, legally, through the political structure. In a little more than a generation the Polynesian natives had overwhelmingly embraced Western culture, along with its style of dress and its religion. There are few practicing Kahunas on the Islands today, but I have had opportunities to meet the most powerful.

I came in contact with Max Freedom Long in 1968. He, of course, was the grand old man of Kahuna magic. He sent me package after package of books and tapes and notes and clippings, and he shared with me many of the secrets that he had accumulated in his research, which began at the turn of the century.

When I was first in Hawaii, in February of 1972, I was able to meet Kahunas such as the Reverend Eddie Kung, who is the son of a Kahuna who had great healing powers; Sam Loma, a Huna priest; and a woman of great power named Morna Simeona. I listened to tale after tale of how Kahuna magic had proved time and again to be too powerful for such modern mechanisms as sparkplugs and internal combustion engines. I heard how mysterious things would keep interfering with the work of the bulldozers on sacred ground – how even state officials had grown impatient trying to confront the power of Kahuna priests.

Today most of the Kahunas have gone underground. There are a few who perform showy rituals, just as in New Orleans there are Voodoo priests who do certain dances and certain rituals for the tourists. These performances are a pale reflection of the authentic.

Essential to the understanding of Kahuna magic is the belief that each human being has three souls or spirits that reside within. These three souls, or spirits, the Kahunas call the *Unihipili*, the *Uhane*, and the *Aumakua*.

The *Unihipili* correlates to the subconscious in modern psychology. The *Uhane* and the *Unihipili* are two separate spirits that inhabit one body. The two spirits work as a team. Each has functions that rely on the abilities of the other, and each needs the physical medium of the human body.

The *Aumakua* translates literally as the older, parental, clearly trustworthy pair – meaning that it is composed of a male and female essence, a balance and a polarity that is necessary for working any magical system on the earthly plane. This dual spirit has both the lower self, the *Unihipili*, and the middle self, *Uhane*, under its guidance and protection. It occupies the level of consciousness immediately above our own conscious level , and it corresponds to the superconscious in psychology.

The *Aumakua*, called the high self, is the highest god with whom the Kahunas ever dealt. They believed in the supreme creative force, but they did not believe that they could pray to it or appease it. The only level of consciousness that they felt they could humanly comprehend was the one in which they were dwelling. Their only contact with a level directly above their own was due to their connection with the high self, the *Aumakua*.

The other essential element in understanding Kahuna magic, is that of the *Aka* substance. According to Kahuna belief, surrounding these three spirits – or selves – within each human are three invisible or shadowy bodies. These shadowy selves correspond to the etheric and the astral doubles of occult literature. These amorphous bodies are made up of what the Kahunas called the *Aka*.

The *Aka* substance formed the sheath or the cloak in which the three souls could reside. There was one sheath for each respective soul, with varying degrees of intensity.

The *Aka* substance is said to be "sticky" in Kahuna magic, thereby explaining how one can touch an object and symbolically connect to the *Aka* thread that is still bound in the spirit substance to the person who has owned that object before. The spirit self within the medium travels the *Aka* thread to gain information about the previous owner of whatever object is being held.

Another essential item in understanding Kahuna is that of the *Mana*. The *Mana* is a vital force which reposes in the human body. It is the low self that produces simple *Mana*. The middle self uses *Mana-mana,* Mana with a "higher voltage," so to speak. The high self uses *Mana-loa*. The electromagnetic voltage used by the high self is so supercharged that it has extraordinary properties, literally able to smash atoms of reality.

As we learn more about our world, we see that everything is energy, everything vibrates and everything is one form or another of a manifestation of the electromagnetic spectrum.

In his early research, Max Freedom Long presumed that these voltages were electrical. Low *Mana* could be likened to the body waves, which have been recorded scientifically in the laboratory. *Mana-mana* may correspond to the brain waves, and *Mana-loa* could find its counterpart in what other traditions speak of as the *Chi,* the *Ki,* the Holy Spirit, the *Wakan-tonka* – that vital substance that inhabits and moves through every living thing and can be focused by the human psyche literally to create miracles.

The most essential element necessary for success in Kahuna magic is contact with a high self. It is on this level, above our own conscious level, that the power is sufficient to perform physical miracles. The Kahuna thought that contact with the superconscious could only be made by the low self, acting under orders from the middle self. The low self is connected to the high self by a shadowy cord, the *Aka,* made of the same substances as the shadowy bodies. When contact is desired, it is achieved by the flow of *Mana* up the *Aka* until the high self is reached.

Now, unfortunately, especially for beginners, it is not unusual for some sort of blockage to appear, making contact very difficult. The blockage, unless it is caused by the intervention of the external spirit, usually occurs on the subconscious level.

The low self, it was believed by the Kahunas, served as the seat of memory, in which all the thought forms that have been created by the middle self are stored.

You must remember, also, that in the Kahuna system thoughts really are things. Each thought literally becomes a tiny bead of *Aka* substance that clusters around the other thoughts of a similar nature.

When you require a specific piece of information, your middle self simply instructs your low self to produce the necessary information. The whole cluster of *Aka* beads are reviewed, explaining in Kahuna terms why memory is associational.

The low self is the creator of emotions. Within it are formed such emotional responses as fear and guilt and pride.

It is guilt, however, and all those emotions that are associated with it that most concern us as visionaries, for those are the emotions that can inhibit contact with the high self. If the low self does something of which it is ashamed, it will try to avoid the high self, much as the naughty child stricken with remorse or fear of punishment, will seek to avoid its parents.

Guilt and fear can become fixed thought forms in the low self. Every time the middle self instructs the low self to contact the high self, it can collide with those emotions and be unable to make contact. We see, then, in terms of the Kahuna cosmology, why an individual may often find him- or herself at the mercy of the unreasonable subconscious self.

In our modern society an individual faced with such a problem will go to a psychoanalyst. In Hawaii years ago (and in some cases *today* – if one knows where to acquire a Kahuna priest) one would go to a Kahuna to solve such a problem.

Of special use to those who would create positive tomorrows is the utilization of the great *Ha* prayer rite. It was the correct use of the *Ha* prayer rite that enabled ancient Kahunas to contact that intangible energy (the X-force, the Unknown Energy) that answers prayers – and from the human perspective, literally performs miracles.

The Huna prayer rite works because the high self has the ability to change the future. This is what prayer is all about. If you wish to change a certain condition it is because you are convinced that certain undesirable factors show no signs of changing themselves, but will continue a negative course into the future.

The high self builds the future for you, using your mental images as its tools. That is why the proper formulation of goals is so important. Obviously, if a consistent image is projected, a consistent future will be constructed.

Once you employ this future-changing ability of the high self, you will carefully choose the correct prayer, and faithfully repeat it every day.

It is necessary to be able to reach the high self to perform any type of magic, and this rite can be used by anyone who earnestly desires to establish that type of contact. If you correctly follow this format and practice it, you will be able to accomplish the same kind of feats of telepathy, clairvoyance and prophecy that the Kahunas did regularly in earlier times – and still do in secret today.

There are four basic steps in the *Ha* prayer rite; but before mentioning them, two additional elements must be stressed. These are consistency and repetition. It is important that the high self receives a clear and unwavering picture of the situation or the object that you desire through your prayer. If the high self picks up the contradictions and fragments of a constantly changing image, it will be confused.

In order to keep the image as clear as possible, you should carefully choose the prayer that you wish to make.

You should know in advance which image you intend to send to your higher self. If you have done the work of deciding these things before the actual work of your prayerful undertaking, you should not have to worry about sending a confused request.

Here are the four basic steps in performing the *Ha* prayer rite:

First, the middle self will instruct the low self to create an extra amount of *Mana*. This is done by taking four deep breaths. These breaths should be taken in very slowly, and the breathing should be deep and regular. Once the *Mana* or the vital force has been aroused, it is held in readiness.

With the accumulated *Mana* still residing in the lower self, the subconscious reaches up along the shadowy *Aka* cord until the high self has been successfully contacted.

When this contact is assured, the low self releases its store of *Mana* in a kind of sacrificial gift to the high self. The high self will use its vital force to formulate the answer to the prayer.

Finally, rising up the *Aka* cord with the *Mana* is the mental image of the thing desired by you.

The repetition of this rite is so necessary that it should be considered a fifth step. And not only should the clear picture be continually projected, but so should the daily supply of *Mana*. *Mana* strengthens the high self. Without *Mana* the high self would be too weak to accomplish anything in the physical world in which we live.

We have been told in innumerable sources that "whatsoever things you desire, believe that you have them, and you shall have them." The element of belief is of great importance for the successful application of the *Ha* prayer.

Throughout the actual rite, the individual must rest in a quiet faith that the high self is already taking care of the request. Just as one can plant a seed and see it grow into a plant and pick the fruit, so should one envision the path taken by one specific prayer. The seed must eventually be trusted to bear fruit. The length of time involved simply depends on the nature of the request. Some changes, of course, will require considerably more time than others.

In order for a prayer to be successful, you must look to the request and to the motivation. The Kahunas were emphatic in their belief that the high self, the utterly trustworthy, parental pair, could perform no ill to anyone. The two lower selves, regretably, did have this failing. But if they ever chose to harm someone, it was an action divorced from the high self. The *Ha* prayer rite cannot be successfully employed if you seek to harm another, either physically or emotionally.

As I said, the Kahunas believed that thoughts were things, that they were composed of the same *Aka* substance as the three shadowy bodies. Each time you formulate the *Ha* prayer it becomes a microscopic bead on the *Aka* thread. For each repetition a duplicate bead is made, and the stronger becomes the strand. The Kahuna system may actually explain the mechanics of the positive thinking approach, which teaches one constantly to project a positive mental attitude.

The Kahunas believe that the great events of the future are set and can be foreseen far ahead. World or national events might be seen hundreds or even thousands of years ahead. The future of the individual, because of the shortness of the human life span, could be seen only months or years ahead.

The Kahunas often demonstrated their abilities to change the future for the individual, for their most essential belief was that the future was not irrevocable. The future could be changed, they believed; and frequently, it seems they did so.

According to Huna, it is the high self that constructs the future out of the thoughts and imagination of the middle self. This jumble of conflicting desires and fears is related to the high self via the low self most frequently during sleep. The high self then takes those thoughts formed of *Aka* substance and fastens it to a very real future. Just as the physical body sets the mold of the high self's shadowy body, so do events and people fit this future mold created by the high self.

Sleep is the most common time for thought forms to travel up the *Aka* cord to the high self. For in sleep, conscious barriers are lowered and the suggestible sleep consciousness is more easily reached. Anyone desiring to actively influence the thought forms chosen by the high self to be used in forming the future should begin work with the sleep state. The subconscious self is extremely impressionable. It is also incapable of any other than very rudimentary powers of reasoning. If a thought can be lodged in it, the subconscious would be persuaded to hand the thought form over to the high self.

In planning for the future, thoughts lodged in the low self would be the ones used by the high self to build a corresponding future. One method of influencing the future is to imply thought forms in the low self when it is asleep – its most suggestible period. This can be done with tape recorders set to play the desired message to the low self. When the tape recorder is used on a regular basis, the individual will adjust to the disturbance and cease to wake up when the message is played. The advantage of this method is that the message is being relayed to the low self at the time when contact with the high self is most propitious.

After spending a great deal of time with Medicine People from many different tribes in the United States, I have put together what I believe to be the most essential elements of Medicine Power or Native American magic. I realize how presumptuous it is to try to distill the very essence of the cosmology of the many different tribes into eight steps; but it is my opinion that, in spite of the great cultural differences that I found from tribe to tribe, I noticed the same basic elements of spiritual expression. I have broken those elements down this way:

1. The vision quest with its emphasis on self-denial and the spiritual discipline, which is extended to a lifelong pursuit of wisdom of body and soul.

2. A reliance upon one's personal visions and individual dreams to provide one's direction on the path of life.

3. A search for personal songs to enable one to attune oneself to the primal sounds, the cosmic vibration of the Great Spirit.

4. A belief in a total partnership with the world of spirits and in the ability to make a personal contact with grandfathers and grandmothers who have changed planes of existence.

5. The possession of a nonlinear time sense.

6. A receptivity toward the evidence that the essence of the Great Spirit may be found in everything.

7. A reverence and a passion for the Earth Mother, the awareness of one's place in the web of life, and one's responsibility toward all plant and animal life.

8. A total commitment to one's beliefs that pervades every aspect of one's total life and enables one truly to walk in balance.

For several years now I have incorporated my own personal metaphysics with Native American Medicine Power. I find that it is imperative in Native American magic or in any practice of metaphysics to set a time apart to enable one to enter the Silence of deep meditation.

In one sense I do a condensed version of the vision quest. During the course of my day-to-day routine, I have a daily exercise program in which I work vigorously with barbells and dumbells, ride a bicycle and go for a long walk in order to exert my body and distract my conscious self. I find that just as one on a vision quest may deplete the physical self with monotonous and strenuous tasks in order to free the subconscious, so, for me, does the workout with weights accomplish this same goal.

After this period of exercise, I enter a hot shower (which is, in one sense, the counterpart of an instant sweat lodge). After I have towel-dried, I lie flat on my back in a quiet place, apart from everyone and all distractions, and permit easy access in my heightened state of awareness to whatever is to come to me from the silence. For an added physical stimulus, I might wrap myself in a blanket, even covering my head. Such a withdrawal and sealing off increases my sensation of being totally isolated and permits me to become even less aware of my physical body and my surroundings.

One may also smoke as an aid to meditation. Native Americans smoked by way of religious observance, not for personal pleasure. I recommend a very moderate use of tobacco, but as a physical stimulus, one can offer the pipe (I think that cigars and cigarettes would be far less preferable for such a ritual) to the four directions, upward to the Great Spirit, and downward to the Earth Mother.

The puffs of smoke being carried toward the ceiling or the sky should represent one's thoughts or prayers being offered to the Great Spirit. One should use these rhythmically released clouds of smoke as focal points for concentration.

If you have achieved an attitude of calm before smoking, you should find that your thoughts and images will begin to come to you almost at once.

Traditional Medicine People carry a medicine bag, which is filled with objects regarded as personally sacred to the bearer. If you should wish to emulate this practice you should remember to include objects symbolic of the four elements – fire, water, air and earth. And you should remember that these objects (and any other items that may have personal significance to you) serve as physical stimuli upon which you might meditate in order to open the channel of your subconscious.

You might wish to go out, as many Native Americans do, to find your medicine stone. The medicine stone is something you can carry in your bag, or you might drill a hole through it and wear it about your neck on a leather thong, as a kind of physical stimulus.

I believe as did the Native Americans, that my dreams are telling me something about myself that I do not already know. Or that they are revealing patterns, future or present, of which it would be to my advantage to be made aware.

Dream control is difficult, but it is hardly impossible to learn. Anyone can keep dream diaries and maintain a permanent record of the assistance being given nightly by the unconscious. Dream symbols are personal, and while there seem to be universal images, which bear consistently similar messages to dreamers in several cultures, you must come to know yourself during the vision quest, so that you may be able to sort out glimpses of the future from bits and pieces of psychological garbage, which are being manufactured by other levels of consciousness.

During the vision quest or in deep meditation, one often acquires a personal song or sound. This personal vibration will greatly facilitate you in future meditations. If you have not received such a song or sound, don't overlook certain pieces of music, which may contain nostalgic triggers that will work for you, invoking images of great strength.

Nearly everyone has a song that is loaded with particularly sentimental images. Sometimes those melodies can send you back to a particular experience. And then, after that moment has been relived, your unconscious can be soaring here and there and often returning with valuable insights.

Music has the capacity to take you into the past – then allow you to daydream or wander mentally into areas in which your higher self can reach down and bring you up by the hand into greater awarenesses. Music is an ideal way to prime the pump, to get your creative and meditative mechanisms into full operation.

Do not neglect the many fine recordings of Native American music. There have been some recent New Age compositions that combine the traditional with modern recording techniques.

In our modern American society, one may often become rather uneasy in stating a belief in a total partnership with the world of spirits. I think you might begin by at least keeping the door open to the possibility that you may be able to establish contact with those who graduated to other planes of existence. Under no circumstances should the situation be forced. A relaxed and tranquil state of mind will best permit your psyche to soar free of time and space and return with images, impressions, messages. Each session should begin with your asking a prayer for guidance and protection.

One of the most difficult aspects that the modern man or woman has to overcome in truly practicing Kahuna magic, American Indian Medicine, or any system of magic is to learn to live in a nonlinear time sense. Our society is so completely and slavishly governed by the human-made markings of linear time, that we must, through meditation, stop the world and learn how to develop a magic or spiral time sense.

As I have stated repeatedly, meditation affords the most effective method I know for allowing one to break free of the boundaries of conventional time. We must always realize that central to an understanding of any system of magic is the knowledge that, for one level of the unconscious (the deepest and most spiritually attuned level), linear time does not exist. All is an Eternal Now. An altered state of consciousness properly conducted will permit you to enter that time-free, unchartered, measureless kingdom of the psyche.

At the same time, one must establish a close connection to the Earth Mother. One must learn to see and to appreciate all of her adornments and trappings.

You must come to know that you are a part of the universe and that the universe is a part of you. You must recognize that the essence of the Great Spirit is to be found in all things. You must bear your responsibility toward all plant and animal life with dignity and not with condescension. If you can come to feel in touch with an energy source outside of yourself, you will come to feel a new power within your own being.

22

Establishing Good Health Through Color Therapy

In this chapter I am going to present a series of color meditations that can enable you to have health and vigor beyond any physical-mental state that you may have achieved prior to this time. Being mentally prepared for what will occur in the future is only a portion of what you will need. You must be healthy and fit to live the future as fully as you want.

Since these techniques deal with color and with repetitious progressions, it is quite easy to memorize them and to be able to place yourself in an altered state of consciousness. As previously suggested, you may wish to record a cassette of your voice ahead of time, thereby becoming your own guide through the experiences. If you have a likeminded friend or family member to guide you through a complete exercise, so much the better.

You may find it extremely helpful to play a recording of the proper kind of music, which would suggest a mood of lifting away. Any music that you find inspirational will do. Just be certain that the music is instrumental only, for lyrics will distract you and suggest other images than the ones desired.

Sit on a chair, lie on your bed, lean against a wall, whatever position is most comfortable for you. Select a time when you will not be disturbed. Disconnect the telephone, and turn on your music and your cassette recorder.

Restful Sleep

Visualize that at your feet lies a blanket the color of rose. The color of rose stimulates natural body warmth and induces sleep. It also provides one with a sense of well-being and a great feeling of being loved.

Now you see that the blanket is really a kind of auric color, a rose-colored auric cover.

Imagine that you are willing the blanket-like cover of rose to move slowly over your body.

Feel it moving over your feet, relaxing them. Over your legs, relaxing them; over your stomach, removing all tensions; moving over your chest, your arms, your back.

Now as you make a hood of the rose-colored auric cover, imagine that the color of rose permeates your psyche and enables you to achieve perfect health and restful sleep. Once you have done this, visualize yourself bringing the rose-colored aura over your head.

The Proper Building of Muscle and Tissue

The color green serves as a disinfectant and a cleanser. It also influences the proper building of muscle and tissue.

Imagine that you are pulling a green blanket-like aura over your body.

Feel it moving over your feet, cleansing them.

Feel it moving over your legs, healing them of all pains.

Feel it moving over your stomach, ridding it of all tension.

Feel it moving over your chest, your arms, your neck – cleansing them, healing them.

As you make a hood of the green-colored auric cover, imagine that the color green permeates your psyche and insures the proper building of muscle and tissue in your body.

Once you have done this, visualize yourself bringing the green-colored aura over your head.

Strengthening the Nerves and Aiding Digestion

Gold has been recognized as a great strengthener of the nervous system. It also aids digestion and helps you to become calm.

Visualize now that you are pulling a soft, beautiful golden aura slowly over your body.

Feel it moving over your feet, calming you.

Feel it moving over your legs, relaxing them.

Feel it moving over your stomach, soothing any nervous condition.

Feel it moving over your chest, your arms, your neck. As you make a comfortable hood of the golden aura, imagine that the color of gold permeates your psyche and strengthens your nervous system so that your body-brain network will create a healthier and happier individual.

Once you have done this, visualize yourself bringing the gold-colored aura over your head.

Cleansing Your Lungs

Red-orange strengthens and cleanses the lungs.

In our modern society with its problems of pollution, our lungs become fouled, whether we smoke cigarettes or not. Yogis and other masters have long known that effective meditation, effective altered states of consciousness, can only be achieved through proper techniques of breathing through clean lungs.

Visualize before you a red-orange cloud of pure oxygen. Take a comfortably deep breath and visualize some of that red-orange cloud moving into your lungs.

Imagine it traveling through your lungs, cleansing them, purifying them, carrying away particles of impurities.

Now visualize yourself *exhaling* that red-orange cloud of oxygen from your lungs. See how soiled with impurities it is. See how darkly colored it is.

Take another comfortably deep breath. See again the red-orange cloud of pure, clean oxygen moving into your lungs. See the red-orange cloud purifying your lungs, counteracting the negative effects of vehicle exhausts, smoke and industrial gases.

Exhale the impurities, then breathe again the purifying red-orange cloud until you visualize your lungs as cleansed and healthy.

Purifying the Organs and Glands

The color of yellow-orange will aid oxygen in moving into every organ and gland of your body, purifying them, cleansing them.

Imagine before you now a yellow-orange cloud of pure oxygen. Take a comfortably deep breath and inhale that cleansing, purifying yellow-orange cloud into your lungs. Feel the yellow-orange cloud moving through your body. Feel it cleansing and purifying every organ. Feel it cleansing and purifying every gland.

If you have an area of weakness or disease anywhere in your body, feel the yellow-orange energy bathing it in cleansing, healing vibrations.

As you *exhale* all impurities, *inhale* again the pure, clean, yellow-orange cloud of oxygen.

Visualize the cleansing, healing process throughout your body.

As you exhale and inhale, see your body becoming pure and clean. See now that the cloud which you exhaled is as clean and as pure as that which is being inhaled.

You have cleansed and purified your lungs. You have cleansed and purified and healed all of your body and all of its organs.

Lowering Blood Pressure

Visualize that at your feet lies a blanket the color of purple.

The color of purple helps to lower blood pressure and helps to calm the heart. It also provides one with a sense of purpose and resolution.

See that the blanket at your feet is really a kind of auric cover, a purple-colored auric cover.

Imagine that you are willing the blanket-like aura of purple to move slowly up your body.

Feel it moving over your feet, relaxing them; over your legs, relaxing them; over your stomach, easing all tensions; moving over your chest, slowing down the beat of your heart. Feel it relaxing your heart, lowering your blood pressure, then moving over your arms and your neck.

And now as you make a hood of the purple-colored auric cover, imagine that the color of purple is permeating your psyche and lowering your blood pressure, helping you to become a healthier and happier individual.

Once you have done this, visualize yourself bringing the purple-colored aura over your head.

Building Greater Vitality

Visualize that at your feet lies a blanket the color of blue.

In addition to prompting psychic sensitivity, the color of blue stimulates vitality. It also provides one with a sense of accomplishment and confidence.

See that the blanket at your feet is really a kind of auric cover, a blue-colored auric cover.

Imagine that you are willing the blanket-like aura of blue to move slowly up your body.

Feel it moving over your feet, relaxing them.

Over your legs, relaxing them.

Over your stomach, easing all tensions.

Feel it moving over your chest, your arms and your neck.

Everywhere the blue blanket touches you, you feel vitality surging through your body. You feel renewed energy moving throughout every cell of your body.

Now as you make a hood of the blue-colored auric cover, imagine that the color of blue is permeating your psyche and totally building maximum vitality. Feel it giving you vigor to accomplish all of life's important tasks. Feel the color of blue doing its part in activating your complete health and happiness.

Once you have done this, visualize yourself bringing the blue-colored aura over your head.

Stimulating the Senses

Visualize at your feet a blanket the color of red.

The color of red stimulates the senses. It also helps to build confidence.

Visualizing the color of red can enable one to meet difficult tasks and challenges with a renewed sense of purpose and goal.

Now you see that the blanket at your feet is really a kind of auric cover, a red auric cover.

Imagine that you are willing the blanket-like aura of red to move slowly up your body.

Feel it moving over your feet, over your legs, over your stomach, over your chest, your arms, your neck.

As the red-colored blanket moves over your body you feel a very stimulating sensation. It is not a sensation of urgency, not a feeling of alarm, but it is a stimulus, one of a very positive vibration.

Now, as you make a hood of the red-colored auric cover, imagine that the color of red permeates your psyche and raises your confidence, stimulates your senses, and does its part in making you a more complete, healthy and happy individual.

Once you have done this, visualize yourself bringing the red-colored aura over your head.

23

Creating a Positive Approach to Tomorrow's Problems

By no means should you wait until tomorrow to begin to practice the exercises in this chapter. Please start immediately to remove negativity from your life, so that your future will be as positive as you can possibly make it.

Recognize that you are responsible for your actions and your attitudes – then set about programming your mental machinery to deal with each new problem in a manner that transforms crises to challenges.

Blocking Discord from Your Life

When you permit elements of discord to enter your life you limit yourself by your lack of understanding of the polarities of material plane existence. You become your own condemnation when you tightly draw your limitations around you.

The vibratory rate of discord is so slow that you will soon begin to live an existence that will only be a shadow of your full potential.

Perhaps the origin of your discord lies in a rebellious nature. Through repeated applications at inappropriate moments, the facets of rebellion may have grown to discord over a great length of time through a gradual process.

Or maybe your discord has its roots in fear. Jealousy, criticism, condemnation and judgment are all manifestations of a basic fear that you may not be perfect.

Fear can eventually batter down the walls of the strongest mental and spiritual fortress. The implantation of fear is one of the greatest weapons of the discordant energies.

If you should feel discord coming upon you, do the following:

Cross your arms over your solar plexus.

Put your knees or your feet together. If you are sitting, cross your legs.

The above actions instantly symbolize that you are not receptive, you are not open to discord.

If you are in a social situation and you feel that a person present is seeking to bombard you with negativity and discord, move your arms across your solar plexus, cross your knees if seated, then visualize a cross of blue flame dropping between you and the person or the condition that is afflicting you with vibrations or discord.

Such immediate action can block the vicious energy that is being directed at you. In addition, take short breaths for a time, inhaling shallowly, but exhaling in a somewhat forceful manner. This procedure should not be practiced over-long, but with ample time to express your sentiments that you are not even breathing in the negativity that is being broadcast in your direction.

Changing Negative Energy

When the day has been a difficult one, filled with hostile encounters and lots of sharpshooters verbally sniping at you, go to your personal place — whether it is your bedroom or a clearing in a forest — and practice the following exercise:

Bend your elbows and lift your hands, palms outward to the level of your chest. Take a comfortably deep breath, then emit the universal sound of "OM" in a long drawn-out chant: O-O-O-O-M-M-M.

Repeat this until you are able to feel the energy tingling in the palms of your hands. This is a good exercise for raising both your vibrations and your spirit.

Once you feel more positive, bring your palms toward one another until you are able to feel the Life Energy as a palpable "substance" between them. Focus upon this energy.

Visualize the energy moving upward from your palms to your fingers. Feel it moving up your arms, your shoulders, your neck, your face. Imagine the energy feeding new life, new "blood" to your entire physical being.

Utter the universal sound of "OM" once again. Visualize the energy moving up to your head then cascading down in sparks of golden light, as if you were being enveloped by the downward pouring of a roman candle.

Impress upon your consciousness that those "sparks" represent new, positive energy that is descending around your physical body and forming a vital protective shield against discord and negativity.

Let us say that you have been bombarded with negativity by a vicious person or by a situation that has left you feeling rather defeated and very much alone in the world. Perhaps you are away from home, and you feel that everyone in that strange environment is against you.

Go to a room or to a place where you can be alone to re-establish your emotional and spiritual equilibrium. Sit quietly for a moment. If possible, play some soft, restful music.

After you have begun to calm yourself, say, as you *inhale,* "I am." On the *outbreath,* say, "relaxed."

Repeat this process a number of times. Take comfortably deep breaths: *"I am,"* asserting your sovereignty and your individual reality on the intake; *"relaxed,"* positively affirming your calm condition on the outtake.

Now visualize someone you know or whom you love who is extremely positive and who shares your philosophy, your perspective, your point of view about life and the cosmos. This may be a spouse, a friend, a business associate, a teacher.

See the person on whom you are focusing turning toward you with a smile of love. See the person extending his or her hand to yours.

Feel the touch of fingertip to fingertip. Sense the electrical crackle of energy moving between you. Experience the warmth of the love that flows from entity to entity.

Visualize your taking that person's hand in your own. Feel comfortable knowing that there is one who loves you and who exhibits concern for you.

See this shared love erecting a barrier between you and the negative bombardment to which you have been subjected that day.

Next imagine you or your friend reaching forth a hand to take another's. Visualize yet another like-minded man or woman who is being welcomed to your circle. See that person joining you, smiling as he or she takes a place beside you to add to your fortress of bonded energy.

Continue to imagine other men and women joining your circle until you have built as large a barrier as you feel that you need to face the hostility or the negativity that is being directed against you in this strange and unfamiliar environment. Feel strength, born of love, swell within your breast.

Visualize energy moving from member to member of your magic circle. See the Golden Light of Protection encircling your group externally. See the energy of unconditional love flowing from one to another as you imagine yourself holding hands and linking your vibratory frequency to that of others of your spiritual philosophy.

When you have become completely fortified and calmed, it would be best to go to bed and enjoy a peaceful night's rest.

If this is impossible and you must return to the encounter, know that you will do so totally prepared and reinforced for any situation that might arise. Stride confidently into the "arena," knowing that you are linked together in an unbreakable bond of love with those kindred souls who share your perspective and your goals.

Before you judge whether an event in your life was negative or "evil," try to permit a certain amount of time to pass so that you might assess the experience from a more complete perspective. Because of hurt, embarrassment, or anger, we often cannot see the total picture. As time passes, we may be better able to accept the negative experiences as an event of growth, an opportunity for an expansion in awareness.

How unfortunate it is that we so often allow our emotions to dictate our interpretation of an event. Emotional pain frequently shuts our eyes to the proper assessment of the lesson and the learning received from what we have so readily judged as a negative experience.

We actually grow by enduring and seeing through to the end those experiences that are difficult. With the passage of time, after the damaged emotions have been healed and the heated passions have been cooled, we may be able to view the event with a much clearer and much more enlightened perspective. What at first might have been regarded as a curse can more clearly be perceived as a blessing in disguise – a blessing that has permitted us to gain greatly in awareness, thus raising our vibratory frequency.

The essence of this chapter is that the one certain thing that can always correct imbalance, negativity and evil is unconditional love channeled through the Higher Self. Darkness must always yield to Light.

When you vibrate with the highest frequency of unconditional love for all living things, you resonate with the harmony of the Heavens. All positive teachings and awareness will be given to you.

I hope that you have already noticed that when you give unconditional love, its energy can never be depleted, for you receive it anew from Above. You can never receive imbalance, hatred, envy, or jealousy when you are filled with love. You can never be touched by negative vibrations when you are filled with love.

Neither can you fill yourself with love and hold it within your being. You must pour it forth upon the world or it will stagnate. Love must be given so that you may receive it afresh.

Truly giving and receiving love is the true way to create and maintain the balanced and peaceful tomorrow we all desire. The weather cycles indicate that our near future will be extremely difficult. We will only be able to overcome these difficult times by maintaining an individual balance and spirituality and by broadcasting that to each person we meet. This is the way in which we will create the tomorrow we all desire, and this is the purpose for which the exercises in this book were designed.

ASTRAL PROJECTION

Brad Steiger

Parapsychological researchers have established that one of every one hundred persons has experienced out-of-body projection (OBE). These experiences are not limited to any single type of person, but rather they cross all typical boundaries.

In *Astral Projection*, Brad Steiger investigates the phenomenon of OBE and correlates those events into broad categories for analysis and explanation. In his clear and non-sensational style, Steiger relates how these spontaneous experiences occur and when they are likely to re-occur. In addition to the standard and well-documented categories of spontaneous astral projection at times of stress, sleep, death and near-death, Steiger devotes considerable time to the growing evidence for conscious out-of-body experiences, where the subject deliberately seeks to cast his or her spirit out of the physical shell.

Along with his study of astral projection, Steiger sets guidelines for astral travellers, tells them the dangers they may face and how this type of psychic experience might be used for medical diagnosis, therapy and self-knowledge.

Author Brad Steiger is your guide to controlling astral projection and using it for your own benefit.

ISBN 0-914918-36-2
234 pages, 6½″ x 9¼″, paper $12.95

A reporter's encounters with ghosts who walk, speak, move objects and even kill. How spirits haunt the scenes of their violent death. Here's convincing proof of a spirit world that exists all around us. With an introduction by Hans Holzer.

Brad Steiger

TRUE GHOST STORIES

A Psychic Researcher's Hunt for Evidence of Hauntings

Brad Steiger

Brad Steiger's years of research into the infinite expanse of the spirit world is now available in this fascinating compilation of verified hauntings. These are not only the classic ghostly manifestations often discussed in paranormal literature, but also cases Steiger has researched, often using well-known mediums as contact points with the ethereal energies. *True Ghost Stories* does not stop at just relating the details of ghostly hauntings, it goes beyond other books on ghosts and hauntings to present the prevailing hypotheses about spirits in a scientific, yet highly readable manner.

    The author investigates and explains three predominant theories that claim such manifestations are "telepathic infection," "idea patterns" or "psychic ether." Steiger concludes that no single one of these theories should be held dominant, but then again, none should exclude the other. *True Ghost Stories* proves the existence of ghosts and reveals significant facts and features of their nature. This new book leaves the reader with the chilling realization that we have yet to fully understand ghosts; more can be learned only through future contacts with the spirits.

ISBN 0-914918-35-4
168 pages, 6½" x 9¼", paper

$7.95

KAHUNA MAGIC

Brad Steiger

Based on the life work of Max Freedom Long, *Kahuna Magic* lays open the secrets of the Kahuna, the ancient Hawaiian priests. Long used the secrets of the Hawaiian language to unlock the secrets of this powerful and mystical discipline.

Long was a much-respected psychic researcher. His student Brad Steiger chronicles Long's adventures on the way to understanding the magic of the Kahuna. By following Long's trek, the reader will learn how the Kahunas used their magic for both the benefit of their friends and the destruction of their enemies.

Central to the Huna beliefs was the thesis that each person has three selves. The Low Self is the emotive spirit, dealing in basic wants and needs. The Middle Self is the self operating at the everyday level. The High Self is the spiritual being that is in contact with every other High Self.

The subject matter of *Kahuna Magic* is contemporary and compelling. The book incorporates many of the concepts and concerns of the modern Western psychological tradition of Jung and Freud while bringing in subjects as diverse as Eastern philosophies and yoga in a manner that will help the readers understand themselves and those around them.

ISBN 0-914918-34-6
127 pages, 6½" x 9¼", paper $10.95

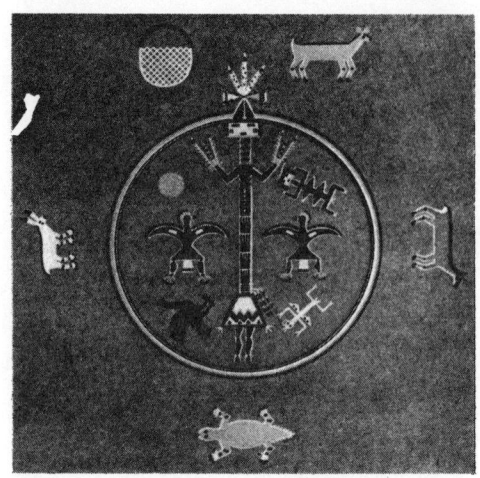

INDIAN MEDICINE POWER

Brad Steiger

According to Brad Steiger, medicine power, a way of life elemental to Native American heritage and contemporary religious practice, may well be the unique mystical experience and the proper spiritual path for our continent. At the core of medicine power is the quest for wisdom of mind and body. Men and women pursuing this quest are often great healers, but the true meaning of the term "medicine" extends beyond the arts of healing to include clairvoyance, precognition and unity with nature and the great spirit.

Indian Medicine Power includes extensive interviews with contemporary medicine men and women from numerous tribes. Steiger himself was initiated into the medicine lodge of the Wolf Clan of the Seneca tribe, given the name of Hat-yas-swas (He Who Testifies) and charged with the search and sharing of universal truths.

The truths of medicine power shared in this book include the nature and importance of the vision quest, the belief in total partnership with the World of Spirits, awareness of one's place in the web of life and the power of walking in balance with the earth.

As Donna Linstead, a member of the Cree Tribe and professor of Native American Studies, says in her introduction: "*Indian Medicine Power* provides each reader with a path from yesterday to tomorrow that allows for individual growth, awareness, and an accessibility to the ancient mysteries that continue to be practiced today. Brad Steiger has demonstrated an uncommon insight into the sacred belief systems of the Amerindian."

ISBN 0-914918-65-6
240 pages, paper

$12.95

HUNA: A Beginner's Guide

Revised Edition
Enid Hoffman

As author Enid Hoffman recalls, "I began to feel with rising excitement that I was on to something very valuable and real. I learned that this concept was at the bottom of all the practices of the Kahuna. Their miracles and magic were the result of their profound knowledge of energies and substances, visible and invisible. This knowledge enabled them to control their life experiences instead of having events control them, and made it possible for them to assist others to do so. I became aware that they were expert psychologists with a thorough understanding of human nature. Their understanding of interpersonal relationships and relationships between the selves and the physical world gave them incredible power.

"For me, these were very exciting realizations, holding the potential for everyone to grow in knowledge and power. My enthusiasm grew because I knew that if the Kahuna had done it, we could do it by studying the Huna concept, practicing their techniques until we were as skilled as they. Then we would be able to produce miracles, too."

Centuries ago, the Kahuna, the ancient Hawaiian miracle workers, discovered the fundamental pattern of energy-flow in the universe. Their secrets of psychic and intrapsychic communication, refined and enriched by modern scientific research, are now revealed in this practical, readable book. Learn to talk directly to your own unconscious selves and others. It could change your life.

ISBN 0-914918-03-6
220 pages, 6½" x 9¼", paper $12.95

EXPAND YOUR PSYCHIC SKILLS

Enid Hoffman

In this sequel to her best-selling *Develop Your Psychic Skills*, Hoffman shows you how to use your inate psychic abilities to improve your daily life and your relationships with other beings. Huna concepts, along with dozens of techniques, exercises, games and meditations are included to help you fully utilize your inner resources. Psychic healing, working with crystals and gemstones, communicating telepathically with people and animals, heightening creative powers, and eliminating old behaviors that are interfering with your personal growth are just a few of the areas covered.

ISBN: 0-914918-72-9
144 pages, 6½" X 9¼", paper

$9.95

DEVELOP YOUR PSYCHIC SKILLS

Enid Hoffman

Psychic skills are as natural to human beings as walking and talking and are much more easily learned. Here are the simple directions *and* the inside secrets from noted teacher and author Enid Hoffman.

Develop Your Psychic Skills gives you a broad overview of the whole field of psychic experiences. The exercises and practices given in this book are enjoyable and easy to do. Use them to strengthen and focus your own natural abilities and turn them into precise, coordinated skills. You'll be amazed at the changes that begin to happen in your life as you activate the right hemisphere of your brain, the intuitive, creative, psychic half, which has been ignored for so long.

This book shows you how your natural psychic powers can transform your life when you awaken the other half of your brain. It teaches you techniques for knowing what others are doing, feeling and thinking. You can see what the future holds and explore past lives. You can learn to locate lost objects and people. You can become a psychic healer. It is all open to you.

Develop occasional hunches into definite foreknowledge. Sharpen wandering fantasies and daydreams into clear and accurate pictures of events in other times and places. Choose what you want to do with your life by developing your psychic skills. When you finish this book you'll realize, as thousands of others have using Enid Hoffman's techniques, that the day you began to develop your psychic skills was the day you began to become fully conscious, fully creative and fully alive.

ISBN 0-914918-29-X
183 pages, 6½" x 9¼", paper, $9.95

COMPLETE RELAXATION

Steve Kravette

Complete Relaxation is unique in its field because, unlike most relaxation books, it takes a completely relaxed approach to its subject. You will find a series of poetic explorations interspersed with text and beautifully drawn illustrations designed to put you in closer touch with yourself and the people around you. *Complete Relaxation* is written for all of you: your body, your mind, your emotions, your spirituality, your sexuality—the whole person you are and are meant to be.

As you read this book, you will begin to feel yourself entering a way of life more completely relaxed than you ever thought possible. Reviewer Ben Reuven stated in the *Los Angeles Times*, "*Complete Relaxation* came along at just the right time—I read it, tried it; it works."

Some of the many areas that the author touches upon are: becoming aware, instant relaxation, stretching, hatha yoga, Arica, bioenergetics, Tai chi, dancing, and the Relaxation Reflex.

Mantras, meditating, emotional relaxation, holding back and letting go, learning to accept yourself, business relaxation, driving relaxation.

Family relaxation, nutritional relaxation, spiritual relaxation, sensual relaxation, massage and sexual relaxation. *Complete Relaxation* is a book the world has been tensely, nervously, anxiously waiting for. Here it is. Read it and relax.

ISBN 0-914918-14-1
320 pages, 6½" x 9¼", paper, $10.95

COMPLETE
MEDITATION

Steve Kravette

Complete Meditation presents a broad range of metaphysical concepts and meditation techniques in the same direct, easy-to-assimilate style of the author's best-selling *Complete Relaxation*. Personal experience is the teacher and this unique book is your guide. The free, poetic format leads you through a series of exercises that build on each other, starting with breathing patterns, visualization exercises and a growing confidence that meditation is easy and pleasurable. Graceful illustrations flow along with the text.

   Complete Meditation is for readers at all levels of experience. It makes advanced metaphysics and esoteric practices accessible without years of study of the literature, attachment to gurus or initiation into secret societies. Everyone can meditate, everyone is psychic, and with only a little attention everyone can bring oneself and one's circumstances into harmony.

   Experienced meditators will appreciate the more advanced techniques, including more sophisticated breathing patterns, astral travel, past-life regression, and much more. All readers will appreciate being shown how ordinarily "boring" experiences are really illuminating gateways into the complete meditation experience. Whether you do all the exercises or not, just reading this book is a pleasure.

   Complete meditation can happen anywhere, any time, in thousands of different ways. A candle flame, a daydream, music, sex, a glint of light on your ring. In virtually any circumstances. *Complete Meditation* shows you how.

ISBN 0-914918-28-1
309 pages, 6½" x 9¼", paper $12.95